I WANT TO BE LEFT BEHIND

an in depth look into the rapture

Pastor Ron Poch

Isaiah 4:3 And it shall come to pass, that he that is **left** in Zion, and he that **remaineth** in Jerusalem, shall be called holy…

 Liberty Press

I Want To Be Left Behind
Written by: Pastor Ron Poch

Published by:
Liberty Press
Post Office Box 339
Adrian, Michigan 49221

Distributed by:
Arrows of Truth
Post Office Box 108
Kennesaw, Georgia 30144

Unattributed quotations are by Ron Poch.

ISBN, print ed.   09719119-1-6

First printing 2002

Acknowledgements

The task of placing this book in your hands is certainly not the work of one person. The labor of love in typing the text could not have been done without the help of Leena Wood, Cathy Beckom and my wife, Sharon. Also I would like to thank Paul Slusser for the cover design, layout and technical support for the completion of this book.

I am indebted to many in our fellowship at North Atlanta Praise for their constructive critique and their love for truth.

Much of the material you read in this book
are from messages preached by Pastor Ron Poch,
hence the style of presentation.

Contents

Foreword

The purpose in sharing this book with you is not to rehash information that has already been put in print and readily available. It was not compiled to cause anger or argument, although it may.

My desire is to have you take a look at *I Thessalonians 4:16-17* in a different perspective and see an aspect that perhaps you previously have not entertained or envisioned. This scripture in *I Thessalonians* is the premier and primary text that preachers, teachers, and evangelists use as proof of the rapture. But what if the verses are really saying something else? The book encourages the reader to question his belief system, which is healthy. It serves to substantiate, in brief form, where the "rapture teaching" got its start, but this is not my aim or intention.

I have asked in prayer for the Lord to give me the "fragments." You remember reading in the Gospels the feeding of the 5,000. Do you recall what our Savior told the disciples in *John 6:12*? He said, *"Gather up the fragments that remain, that nothing be lost."* This really is the "fragment" ministry." I asked God to give me the leftovers that no one else wanted. He's been faithful to do that. The first half of the book deals with the "loaves and fishes" that may have been shared with you before. The last half deals with "fragments of truth" that perhaps will help you in the days to come.

Remember these words: SHOUT…TRUMPET…CAUGHT UP! Read on.

Your friend,

Ron Poch

Introduction

It seems that everyone is interested in prophecy. By this I mean it's not just church attendees, but those who are unchurched. They read 'The Celestine Prophecies," Nostradamus, Edgar Cayce and Jeanne Dixon. There is an innate fascination with the future.

Do you think that the message of prophecy is a grim and appalling destructionist mentality? Is prophecy given to declare disastrous misfortunes that are mind numbing and loathsome? Is prophecy given to awaken us to tremendous tribulation and trouble on every side? I do not see this as God's initial purpose.

God is the Author of prophecy. Let me quote just three portions of scripture that verify this and then we will proceed to the primary purpose of prophecy.

Isaiah 44:6-7, 'Thus saith the Lord, the King of Israel, and his redeemer, the Lord of hosts: I am the first, and I am the last, and beside me there is no God." Verse 7, "And who, as I, shall call, and shall declare it and set it in order for me, since I appointed the ancient people? And the things that are coming, and shall come, let them show unto them."

Isaiah 45:21, "Tell ye, and bring them near; yea, let them take counsel together. Who hath declared this from ancient time? Who hath told it from that time? Have not I, the Lord? And there is no God else beside me, a just God and a savior; there is none beside me."

II Peter 1:19, 21, "We have also a more sure word of prophecy, unto which ye do well that ye take heed, as unto a light that shineth in a dark place, until the day dawn, and the day star arise in your hearts;" Verse 21, "For the prophecy came not at any time by the will of man, but holy men of God spoke as they were moved by the Holy Spirit."

These passages adequately prove that God is the One who authored prophecy. Prophecy is given to reveal the nature of God and His holiness. But the primary purpose of prophecy is about Jesus, not the antichrist. It's all about Him. It's all about His Kingdom. There are allied purposes in prophetic passages that of course warn nations and peoples about desolations and penalties for violating God's Word. But the Biblical perspective that I desire for you to keep in mind is found in *Acts 10:38, 43, "How God anointed Jesus of Nazareth with the Holy Spirit, and with power; who went about doing good, and healing all that were oppressed of the devil; for God was with Him." Verse 43. "To Him (Jesus) GIVE ALL*

THE PROPHETS WITNESS (emphasis added), *that through His name whosoever believeth in Him shall receive remission of sins.* " That's it... remission of sin by His cleansing blood! You are part of a new creation!

My intention and desire is to give all attention and glory to Him for that is the ultimate purpose of prophecy. I pray that I cause no little one offense (*Luke 17:2*) as you read, "I WANT to be Left Behind." But for those of you that are seasoned in the Word, I hope your imagination is throttled and your sensibility rattled by shaking your theological bush. Just eat the grapes and spit out the seeds.

"Magna est veritas et prevalebit"

(Truth is mighty and will prevail)

Chapter 1

God's Purpose – He Will Take You Through

Why in the world would anyone want or desire to be "left behind" when the overwhelming majority of Christians today want to leave? Consider the Gospel songs that evoke tears and pull at our emotions – "I've Got Leaving on My Mind" or "I'll See You in the Rapture," and countless others. Sugarcoated Christianity and spoiled-brat theology, more on this later, doesn't hold up under careful examination of the majority of scripture. Why train an "army of the Lord" to fight and take back all that Satan and his minions have stolen from us nationally and personally if in the "battle of the ages," we get taken up and carried away to some banquet table to eat for three and one-half to seven years, as some prophecy experts expostulate? Are we so weak and puny that our theology or tradition demands that we evacuate the planet and let the devil's crowd take over? Why, I thought the *"earth is the Lord's and the fullness thereof."* (*Psalms 24:1*)

Was the "Rapture" a Teaching of the Early Church?

Do you really think that Jesus suffered and died on Calvary to give the world to the antichrist? That is certainly not the message of the power of the cross and the resurrection. It wasn't the message of the early church! O.K., you say, but let's get back to the title of the book. Why would anyone even consider the thought, "I want to be left behind?" Here's why. *Isaiah 4:2-3* states, *"In that day shall the Branch of the Lord be beautiful and glorious and the fruit of the earth shall be excellent and splendid for those who are escaped of Israel* (survivors). Please get your Bible and read *Verse 3*. It declares, *"And it shall come to pass that he who is <u>left</u> in Zion and he who <u>remaineth</u> in Jerusalem shall be called holy, even every one that is written among the living in Jerusalem."*

Do you want to be called holy? "Of course," you say. Why, that is what Peter exhorted us to be in *1 Peter 1:15-16, "But as He who hath called you is holy, so be ye in all manner of conversation." Verse 16, "because it is written, BE YE HOLY for I am HOLY"* (emphasis added). Peter was quoting from *Leviticus 19:2* which says, *"Speak unto all the congregation of the children of Israel and say unto them YE SHALL BE HOLY* (emphasis added*) for I the Lord your God, am Holy."* (Also *Leviticus 11:44*) All right, what does that prove? Well, at least it proves what Isaiah said, *"He who is left, and he who remains shall be called holy."* When the popular preachers and T.V. evangelists bring their message of escape and declare, "Don't worry, the antichrist, beast, and false prophet will have taken over the world but thank God, we won't be here, we will have been raptured," that's the time for you to stand up and shout "I DON'T WANT TO LEAVE – I WANT TO BE LEFT BEHIND!!!"

What Does "Unorthodox" Mean?

Can you imagine the consternation and frustration your cry would create? Heresy! Oh really? False doctrine! Are you sure? Unorthodox! Well, maybe. But that doesn't mean false. Unorthodox simply means an opinion that is not shared by the majority of the population. It means that at the turn of the twentieth century, Orville and Wilbur Wright would have been unorthodox with their flying machine. They certainly were in the minority insisting that man would be able to fly in a mechanical machine. Yes, they were very unorthodox but were they wrong? No! Try walking instead of flying from New York to Los Angeles.

> **He is developing spiritual muscle in you**

Whenever one's beliefs are challenged, most of us become rather defensive instead of investigative. I have said many times to others and myself (myself, because I have been so wrong about so many things) that there is a law that is guaranteed to keep me in ignorance, and that law is condemnation before investigation. If I condemn something before I truly with an open mind investigate it, I will forever be in the dark about that subject. And this is never truer than when discussing Bible prophecy.

I'm sure you know the word "rapture" which is made so popular today by the "LEFT BEHIND" series by Tim LaHaye and the "Late Great Planet Earth" by Hal Lindsay is not found in your Bible. Go ahead and check any reputable Bible concordance. You won't be able to find it. It does not exist. It is a man-made term. It does not have Biblical support. Doesn't it seem like it's worth investigating if what you believe about the future isn't mentioned in the Bible? Let me say at this point that what you believe about the "rapture" is not a salvation issue. It is an important issue and will shape your worldview, but it doesn't affect your salvation. However, it will determine how you prepare for the future. For instance, turn to *Romans 10:9-10*. Many of you have memorized these verses by heart. Quote it with me. *"That if thou shalt confess with thy mouth the Lord Jesus and shalt believe in thine heart that God hath raised Him from the dead, thou shalt be saved."* Did you get that? It doesn't say, *"That if thou shalt confess with thy mouth the Lord Jesus and shalt believe in thine heart the* "rapture" doctrine. No! No! No! That is not the qualifying factor for salvation – whether or not you believe in the "rapture." But you MUST believe in the resurrection. The death, burial, and resurrection of our Savior are essential for knowledge of sins forgiven; so let's put the issue of the "rapture" in its proper perspective.

Let Us Search the Scriptures

God repeatedly invites us and exhorts us to search the scriptures as in *John 5:39, "Search the scriptures for in them ye think ye have eternal life and they are they which testify of me."* Can't we do what Jesus urged us to do? Not urged, but really commanded us to do? Or are we afraid of what we might find? Perhaps we should be like the Bereans spoken of in *Acts 17:11* which states, *"These were more noble than those in Thessalonica in that they received the word with all readiness of mind and searched the scriptures daily whether those things were so."* Are you willing to search? Are you willing to change? Of course you know that you are a product of what you've been taught. Just what if you've been taught wrong? Have you the moral stamina, spiritual courage and intellectual honesty to admit it? And correct it? I'm not asking you to be a hyper-critical spiritual detective with an air of superiority, trying to prove you're right and everyone else wrong. Let's ask some honest questions without proof-texting pat answers or popular opinions. Remember, we're on a quest for Bible truth, not church tradition.

God Will Take You THROUGH, Not Out Of

What has been the method in Biblical history that God has used in the past to develop character, faith, and the graces of the Spirit in His people? Wouldn't you at least agree that it has to do with going through difficulties, tests, and trials to prove what mettle a person is made of? Isn't it in the furnace that swords are forged? Isn't it in the kiln that greenware pottery is made usable? Didn't the Apostle James tell us in *James 1:2, "My brethren count it all joy when you fall into various trials."* He said your reaction should be one of JOY, not evasive maneuvers or avoidance. As a matter of fact, the Apostle Peter takes it a step further when he states in *I Peter 1:6-7, "In this ye greatly rejoice though now for a season, if need be, ye are in heaviness THROUGH* (emphasis added) *manifold trials, that the trial of your faith being much more precious than of gold that perisheth, though it be tried with fire might be found unto praise and honor and glory at the appearing of Jesus Christ."* Notice, if you will, two items of interest. First in *Verse 6*, he talks of great rejoicing and then, heaviness. Why both rejoicing and heaviness? Rejoicing because we're going through, heaviness because we're IN the trial. The answer is because we're going THROUGH, not OUT OF! Then in *Verse 7*, he concludes with praise, honor and glory at the APPEARING of Jesus Christ. Not the DISAPPEARING of the saints!

3

Sure, I believe in the second coming of Christ. I just don't believe in the GOING of the church. Friend, has not our God always taken His people THROUGH? Would you read with me a few verses of scripture that insure and verify that the Mighty covenant keeping Yahweh takes His people THROUGH?

Let's look at *Nehemiah 9:9-11 (KJV)*, *"And didst see the affliction* (tribulation) *of our fathers in Egypt and heardest their cry by the Red Sea." Verse 10, "And didst show signs and wonders against Pharaoh and on all his servants and on all the people of this land for Thou knewest that they dealt proudly against them so didst thou get Thee a name as it is this day." Verse 11, "And Thou didst divide the sea before them so that they* (the righteous) *went THROUGH* (emphasis added*) the midst of the sea on the dry land and their persecutors* (the evil ones) *Thou threwest into the deeps as a stone into the mighty waters."* Who was destroyed? The persecutors – the evil people were destroyed! The righteous were preserved.

I'm not trying to proof text anything here but just show you through the example of Pharaoh and his army, the wicked were removed and the righteous inherited the earth. Let's look at *Psalms 66:6, 10-12 (KJV)* and let it speak for itself. *Verse 6, "He turned the sea into dry land, they went THROUGH* (emphasis added) *the flood on foot, there did we rejoice in Him." Verse 10, "For thou, O God, hast tested us, Thou hast tried us as silver is tried* (in the fire*)." Verse 11, "Thou broughtest us into the net. Thou laidst affliction* (tribulation*) upon our loins." Verse 12, "Thou hast caused men to ride over our heads, we went THROUGH fire and THROUGH water* (emphasis added) *but Thou broughtest us out into a wealthy place."*

Turn next to *Psalms 84:5-7.* The scriptures are the best commentary on themselves. They flow in perfect harmony. *Verse 5, "Blessed is the man whose strength is in Thee; in whose heart are the ways of them." Verse 6, "Who passing THROUGH* (emphasis added) *the Valley of Baca* ("Baca" means weeping) *make it a well* (so someone can drink from your experience); *the rain also filleth the pools." Verse 7, "They go from strength to strength; every one of them in Zion appeareth before God."* God is going to take you <u>through</u> your valley experience, <u>through</u> your sorrow, <u>through</u> those trials blacker than a thousand midnights, so others might slake their thirst in the triumph of God's victory in your life. He is taking you THROUGH, not out of. He is developing spiritual muscle in you.

Let's look at *Psalms 106:7-12, "Our fathers understood not Thy wonders in Egypt, they remembered not the multitude of Thy mercies but provoked Him at the sea, even at the Red Sea." Verse 8, "Nevertheless, He saved them for His name's sake, that He might make His mighty power to be known." Verse 9, "He rebuked the Red Sea also, and it was dried up so that He led them THROUGH the depths and THROUGH* (emphasis added) *the wilderness." Verse 10, "And He saved them from the hand of him that hated them and redeemed them from the hand of the enemy." Verse 11, "And the waters covered their enemies: there was not one of them left."* My point is: whom would you say left? The wicked!! And who remained? God's people! Look at *Verse 12, "Then believed they His Words; they sang His praise."* Why? Because God took them THROUGH! My friend, I know that God is glorified when you co-operate with Him. Your faith is strengthened. Your courage is reinforced. And most importantly, God is magnified and becomes bigger to you as a result of making you an overcomer. More on "Overcomers" later.

When Will the World Believe?

At our fellowship, North Atlanta Praise, we sing a chorus. It goes like this:

> *Stand in the fire, in the fire of God's love.*
> *Stand in the fire, the fire from above.*
> *This fire will purge you, it will melt and refine.*
> *So stand in the fire, until your nature's divine.*
> *For He's changing the nature of you and me,*
> *So that we may live in the heavenlies.*

Let me pose an interrogation. Did our Heavenly Father take the three Hebrew boys, Shadrach, Meshach and Abednego, out of the fiery furnace? No. By the way, who was destroyed? Their enemies! The very men who threw them in the furnace that was heated seven times hotter. I think one of the truths that is often overlooked is this. It took three young men to go THROUGH the fire for the heathen king to see the Lord. The king asked in *Daniel 3:24-25, "Did not we cast three men bound into the midst of the fire? He answered and said, Lo, I see four men loose, walking in the midst of the fire, and they have no hurt; and the form of the fourth is like the Son of God."* Hallelujah! When did the king see the Son of God? When three Hebrew children went THROUGH the fire. When are sinners and the ungodly going to see the Son of God? When you're able to walk through the fiery trials and furnace of affliction; not raptured out but THROUGH.

Does *Isaiah* have any insight into this matter? *Chapter 43:1-2, "But now thus saith the Lord who created thee, Oh Jacob, and He who formed thee, Oh Israel, fear not for I have redeemed thee* (not raptured thee), *I have called thee by Thy name, Thou art mine." Verse 2, "When thou passest THROUGH the waters, I will be with thee, and THROUGH the rivers, they shall not overflow thee: when thou walkest THROUGH* (emphasis added) *the fire thou shalt not be burned; neither shall the flame be kindled upon thee."* What was Isaiah saying? God is taking us THROUGH.

David knew a lot about winning battles and fighting the good fight of faith. He declared in *Psalms 18:27-29. Verse 27, "For Thou wilt save the afflicted people; but will bring down high looks." Verse 28, "For thou wilt light my lamp: the Lord my God will lighten my darkness." Verse 29, "For by Thee I have run THROUGH* (emphasis added) *a troop; and by my God have I leaped over a wall."* Would you define David as an overcomer? Why sure! Did he run away from Goliath? Contrary! He ran toward him and God brought him THROUGH! Face your problems – don't avoid them. Our victory is assured!

Let's see what Jeremiah, the weeping prophet, had to say. *Jeremiah 2:5-6* declares, *"Thus saith the Lord, What iniquity have your fathers found in me, that they are gone far from me and have walked after vanity, and are become vain." Verse 6, "Neither said they, "Where is the Lord that brought us up out of the land of Egypt, that led us THROUGH the wilderness, THROUGH a land of deserts and of pits, THROUGH a land of drought, and of the shadow of death, THROUGH a land that no man passed THROUGH and where no man dwelt?"* (emphasis added). Surely Jeremiah believed God would take His people <u>THROUGH</u>, not out of. Do you know what Jeremiah's commission was? *Jer1:10* says it was six-fold:

#1 – to root out

#2 – to pull down

#3 – to destroy

#4 – to throw down

#5 – to build

#6 – to plant

Do you see the negative aspect of his ministry was twice as much as the positive? It was to root out false doctrines, pull down strongholds of tradition, destroy vain imaginations, and throw down fantasy, folklore, and foolishness. Only after this could he build up in the most holy faith and plant the incorruptible seed of the kingdom. No wonder he was called the weeping prophet. Who wouldn't weep at the emaciated, weak condition of a people who at the first sign of trouble, want to run?

One last Old Testament prophet has something for us to ponder. *Zechariah* paints a picture of great despair and destruction. He says in *Chapter 13: 8-9,*

"And it shall come to pass that in all the land, saith the Lord, two parts of it shall be cut off and die; but the third part shall be left." Who is going to be cut off? The wicked. Who is going to be left? The righteous. That's why I want to be left behind!! *Verse 9, "And I will bring the third part THROUGH* (emphasis added) *the fire, and will refine them as silver is refined, and will test them as gold is tested; they shall call on my name and I will hear them. I will say, "It is My people and they shall say, the Lord is my God."* Obviously, these people are going to go THROUGH the fire and THROUGH the dealings of tribulation. Are you appointed to wrath? Of course not!! Will your faith be tested and tried? I'll let you answer that. But of course, the answer is a resounding, "YES!"

Chapter 2

God's Pruning – He Will Remove Erroneous Beliefs

Before we look into what Jesus said concerning staying or leaving, let me ask you a pertinent question. Were you born right? I mean, with all the right answers? Could it be that in your life you have entertained wrong beliefs about salvation, about the baptism of the Holy Spirit, and about the gifts of the Spirit? Could it be that you have wrong beliefs about the rapture and the teachings of futurism?

What is a belief? It is giving mental assent and your thinking processes over to something you are assured is deserving of trust. A correct and right belief will undergird you and be a foundation for your faith. *Hebrews 11:1 states, "Now faith is the substance of things hoped for* (it's a God substance) *and the evidence of things not seen."* It is evidence – evidence that will stand the laboratory test of truth. How do you acquire faith? Paul the Apostle tells us in *Romans 10:17, "So then, faith cometh by hearing, and hearing by the Word of God."*

I often ask our fellowship in Atlanta a series of questions. "How many of you love the Lord? If you do, raise your hands." Almost every hand is raised. Then I ask, "How many of you that love the Lord are filled with the Spirit?" Again, the response is the same. Then I question them further, "How many of you that love the Lord, and are filled with the Spirit, are joyful most of the time?" They think about it, smile, and then raise their hands. Then the final question, "How many of you that love the Lord, are filled with the Spirit, are happy and joyful most of the time, have stupid thoughts?" Hands are raised and we laugh. I then tell them to turn to one another and say, "You need help!" We seem to enjoy telling one another that someone else needs help. So then I have them turn to one another and tell them, "I need help!" And isn't that the truth? I really do need help. And the Holy Spirit was given to lead us and guide us in all truth!

Tradition or Truth?

If a believer's mind is filled with church tradition, old time religion, fables, and untruths, they become a stronghold against actual truth. You eventually hold on to a false belief and refuse to look at scripture without having on the lens or glasses of church tradition. After all, granddad and great granddad believed it and so will I. If we continue believing in a wrong doctrine, we will effectively erect a stronghold in our mind that cannot be penetrated by truth. You say, "Oh, that's not possible!" I assure you that it is possible! You say, "There's nothing stronger than truth." Oh really? Let's look for a moment at what Jesus our Savior said concerning how strong tradition is. *Matthew 15:1-3, 6, "Then came to Jesus scribes and Pharisees, who were of Jerusalem, saying, Verse 2, "Why do thy disciples transgress the TRADITIONS* (emphasis added) *of the elders? For they wash not their hands when they eat bread." Verse 3, "But he answered and said unto them, "Why do ye also transgress the commandment of God* (the Word of God) *by your tradition?" Verse 6, "Thus have ye made the commandment of God* (the truth) *of none effect by your TRADITION* (emphasis added)." Do you see? TRADITION becomes stronger than truth. Jesus then goes on to say in *Verse 8, "This people draweth nigh unto me with their mouth, and honoreth me with their lips; but their heart is far from me." Verse 9, "But in vain do they worship me, teaching for doctrines the commandments of men."* Vain worship is honoring TRADITION over the Word of God. *Verse 10, "And He called the multitude and said unto them, "Hear and understand."* Jesus was telling them to hear and comprehend! Two verses later, it says the Pharisees were offended. You would be surprised how so many of God's people are offended so easily when you honestly desire to show them a perspective of truth they haven't entertained. What about you?

> **The closer you walk with God, sometimes the more you walk alone.**

Some years ago I was watching a very popular T.V. evangelist preaching on the rapture doctrine from *I Thessalonians 4:16-18* (on which we will give an exegesis later on in the book). It was the usual futuristic interpretation. At the end of the broadcast, he proclaimed "I'll believe this teaching till I die, so those of you that send me any literature opposing this view, I won't read it. My mind's made up. I'll never change!" I turned to my wife and said, "The die is cast. He won't change." Do you know why? Solomon, a very wise man, said in *Proverbs 6:2, "Thou art snared with the words of thy mouth, thou art taken with the words of thy mouth."*

Take a New Mind

Jesus said in *Matthew 12:37, "For by thy words thou shalt be justified, and by thy words thou shalt be condemned."* Powerful, isn't it? What are Solomon and Jesus saying? They are telling us we need to repent. The Greek word for repentance in the New Testament is metanoeo, which means, "to take another mind." Basically, it means to change your mind. About what? About life, about your wife or husband, about God, about tradition. It's an 180° turnaround. Are you willing to examine further? Let's change – not for the sake of change, but for the sake of the truth!

Let go of false beliefs. No one desires to live in deception. The Word of God and the Holy Spirit will allow us to look at the scriptures and truth will set us free. One of the greatest freedoms in the world comes when we reject false beliefs and erroneous teachings. Bind yourself to the truth of God's Word and loose yourself from tradition, and the power of the Holy Spirit will lead you into all truth. Strongholds are broken and your mind is open to receive a greater unveiling of the power of God to keep you in the midst of tribulation.

Do you want to be an overcomer – a person that is a victor and not a victim? Did Jesus have anything to say about overcoming? Did He have anything to say about tribulation? Why, sure he did. In the parable of the sower, the seed, and the soil in *Matthew 13*, He said concerning the seed that was sown in stony ground these words in *Verses 20-21*, *"But he that received the seed into stony places, the same is he that heareth the Word, and immediately with joy receiveth it; Yet he hath not root in himself, but endureth for a while: for when TRIBULATION or PERSECUTION* (emphasis added) *ariseth because of the Word, immediately he is offended."* I pray you're not offended. Read on.

The word used for TRIBULATION here in *Matthew 13:21* is the same Greek word used in *Matthew 24:21, 29-30*. Please look at them with me. *Verse 21, "For then shall be great TRIBULATION* (emphasis added) *such as was not since the beginning of the world to this time nor ever shall be."* Look at *Verses 29-30, "Immediately after the TRIBULATION* (emphasis added) *of those days shall the sun be darkened and the moon shall not give her light and the stars shall fall from heaven, and the powers of the heavens shall be shaken: And then shall appear the sign of the Son of Man in heaven: and then shall all the tribes of the earth mourn, and they shall see the Son of Man coming* (not the going of the saints) *in the clouds of heaven with power and great glory."*

An Important Promise – Do You Want It?

Now read a most important verse, again spoken by the lips of Jesus Himself. After reading this verse, let us draw some conclusions, or at least reason together. Okay? *John 16:33, "These things have I spoken unto you, that in Me ye might have peace. In the world ye shall have TRIBULATION but be of good cheer; I have OVERCOME the world."* (emphasis added).

First of all, He gives us and assures us that there is peace in Him. Then He makes a promise. "In this world ye shall have TRIBULATION." Now the same word translated in *Matthew 13:21* and *Matthew 24:21, 29* is the same word that Jesus promised us here in *John 16*. He said we would have TRIBULATION! What are the chances that if Jesus promised it, we're going to be exclusionary and not have it? How can you avoid what Jesus promised would come your way?

The Greek word for TRIBULATION in these verses and others that I will quote is "thlipsis" which is translated "pressure" and also "affliction." This is what Jesus promised but He also left us with the message while going through tribulation, we were to *"be of good cheer."* Why? He said, *"I have overcome the world."*

Can I pose another question while we're at it? Many of you know *John 17* is the High Priestly prayer of our Wonderful Lord and Savior. Do you think our Heavenly Father is going to answer the prayer of His Only Begotten Son? "Sure," you say. "Of course," you declare! Why even ask such a silly question? Surely the Father is going to answer Jesus' prayer! I'd like to quote the whole chapter. But for the sake of the question at this time we'll read just one verse. Remember now, Jesus is doing the praying. *Verse 15, "I pray NOT that Thou shouldest take them out of the world* (the rapture) *but that Thou shouldest KEEP them from the evil."* (emphasis added). You read the entire chapter.

Now if Jesus prayed that you shouldn't be taken out, I ask you "what are your chances of being taken out? Zero! This will soon lead to another emphasis. Who's leaving and who's staying? Of course, that leads into the title of this book, "I Want to be Left Behind." (More on this later).

Where is the Kingdom?

While probing your former or present doctrine concerning the "last days" or the "future," the question arises and begs to be answered. Where is the kingdom going to be? In the beautiful isle of somewhere? In the clouds? In heaven? Where? In the prayer we call the Lord's Prayer found in *Matthew 6:9-10*, Jesus taught the disciples to pray. *Verse 9, "After this manner therefore pray ye: Our Father who art in heaven, Hallowed by Thy Name. Verse 10, Thy Kingdom come* (where?), *Thy will be done* (where?) *IN EARTH* (emphasis added), *as it is in heaven."* God wants His kingdom to be IN EARTH! God wants His will to be done IN EARTH – just as it is in heaven. We'll find out more about God's plan for the earth, but let's again go back to the word "tribulation."

Do you think Paul the Apostle went through TRIBULATION, and if he did, what was his message to the early church? Let's answer the first question. Did Paul go through tribulation? *II Corinthians 11:23-28, "Are they ministers of Christ?* (I speak as a fool). *I am more; in labors more abundant, in stripes above measure, in prisons more frequent, in deaths often." Verse 24, "Of the Jews five times received I forty stripes, save one."*

Verse 25, "Thrice was I beaten with rods, once I was stoned, thrice I suffered shipwreck, a night and a day. I have been in the deep." Verse 26, "In journeyings often, in perils of waters, in perils of robbers, in perils by my own countrymen, in perils by the heathen, in perils in the city, in perils in the wilderness, in perils in the sea, in perils among false brethren;" Verse 27, "In weariness and painfulness, in watchings often, in hunger and thirst, in fastings often, in cold and nakedness." Verse 28, "Besides those things that are without, that which cometh upon me daily, the care of all the churches."

That should answer the first question: did Paul go through tribulation? The amazing thing is he called it "light affliction." Have we been inoculated with such a mild form of Christianity that we are immune to the real thing? In this day of user-friendly religion and Gospel-lite messages, are there those who go on to drastic discipleship? At the first sign and evidence of persecution, what will you do? We need to grow up and become God's men and women.

Let's answer part two of the question. What was Paul's message to the early church? And, has that message changed? Paul was stoned at Lystra. It is written about in *Acts 14:19, "And there came certain Jews from Antioch and Iconium, who persuaded the people, and having stoned Paul, drew him out of the city, supposing he had been dead."*

They were sure he was dead. No one could survive a beating like that. What happened when a person was stoned? First, the victim had to be convicted of a capital crime. Then the mob would take him and tie him up and lie him down. Next, two or three witnesses would take huge boulders or rocks and throw them down on the head or chest cavity of the accused. If the victim didn't die by their head being crushed, the rest of the mob would pick up stones and make sure the execution was finished. The Bible says in the next verse the disciples gathered around the pile of stones and began to pray. In my sanctified imagination, I can see Paul as prayers are ascending. Out of that pile of rocks, his hand emerges as he responds to the intercession of the saints. Getting up, all bruised, with contusions, cuts, abrasions, beat and bloodied, Paul goes right back into the same town – undaunted and undeterred. What nerve! What a man! What fortitude! And what does he say? *Verse 22, "Confirming the souls of the disciples and exhorting them to continue in the faith and that we <u>THROUGH</u> much <u>TRIBULATION</u>* (there's that word again) *enter into the Kingdom of God."* (emphasis added). He said we enter the Kingdom <u>THROUGH</u> <u>TRIBULATION</u>, not out of it – not evading it! What did he tell the Ephesians church in *Chapter 6:10-13*? He informed us first in *Verse 10*, "We have an <u>ally</u> Jesus, Christ the Warrior. Then he said we have an <u>adversary</u> *(Verses 11-12)* the devil, the opposer.

He concluded by saying we have <u>armor</u> *(Verses 13-14)* for battle and victory. No white flag of surrender, no evacuation to a supper in the sky. Read with me *Verse 11, "Put on the whole armor of God that ye may be able to <u>stand</u> against the wiles of the devil." Verse 12, "For we wrestle not against flesh and blood, but against principalities, against powers, against the rulers of darkness of this world, against spiritual wickedness in high places." Verse 13, "Wherefore, take unto you the whole armor of God, that ye may be able to withstand in the evil day* (tribulation), *and having done all, to <u>stand</u>"* (not <u>leave</u> but <u>stand</u>). My friend, you are being prepared for battle, not retreat.

Tribulation Now, Not Later

Why don't we look at what Paul told the Ephesians church previously in *Eph 3:10-13. Verse 10, "To the intent that <u>NOW</u>* (emphasis added) *unto principalities and powers in heavenly places might be made known by the church the manifold wisdom of God," Verse 11, "According to the eternal purpose which He purposed in Christ Jesus, our Lord." Verse 12, In whom we have boldness and access with confidence by the faith of Him." Verse 13, "Wherefore, I desire that ye faint not at my <u>TRIBULATIONS</u>* (emphasis added) *for you, which is your glory."* Of course, the same Greek word used concerning *Matthew 24:21, 29* is exactly the same word used here. How did the saints receive glory? By Paul's going through these tribulations! Many saints of God really and truly believe the "rapture" is the blessed hope. Not so! *Colossians 1:27 declares "To whom God would make known what is the riches of the glory of this mystery among the Gentiles, which is <u>CHRIST IN YOU THE HOPE OF GLORY</u>."* (emphasis added). Can you grasp what the Apostle is saying? His glory is internalized, to come forth in you, not to abandon the earth, not to withdraw, but to manifest Himself <u>now</u>! There is a fallacy to futurism, which postpones victory to a distant time – around the far off bend in the road. The devil is presented so big as if he is running things. And poor little Jesus, with His rag-tag band of losers, why, they're so pitiful they're no match for Satan. It seems as if we, the church of the living God, have given the devil the powers of omnipotence, omniscience, omnipresence and divinity. Jesus didn't die on Calvary to give the world to the devil!

Somehow, our weak theology concerning things in the future dictates to us to believe that the church, which God has been working with for 2000 years, just can't make it. Factor in we've had the power of the Spirit, the gifts of the Spirit (which are the power tools) to produce the fruit of the Spirit. Jesus said in *Matthew 16:18-19, "I will build <u>My</u> Church and the gates* (governments) *of hell <u>SHALL NOT</u> prevail against it."* What has He given to the church? Look at *Verse 19, "And I will give unto thee the keys of* *the kingdom of heaven: and whatsoever thou shall bind on earth, shall be bound in heaven; and whatsoever thou shalt loose on earth, shall be loosed in heaven."*

Does this sound to you like the church is an afterthought in the mind of God? The so-called prophecy experts call the church a "parenthesis." Can you believe it? That which is the masterpiece of the ages, designed by God Himself to be His body, to be His representatives, His ambassadors, His glory in the earth, to have dominion, is called by Darby, Larkin, Scofield, Van Impe and Hal Lindsay (to name a few) a "parenthesis." Here's what is most appalling of all! They tell us when the so-called "rapture" occurs, the church will be gone and the Holy Spirit withdrawn. Then God is going to use 144,000 Jews who are going to be 144,000 evangelists like Billy Graham, heralding again animal sacrifice (which is an insult to the blood of Jesus) and the Jewish temple will be rebuilt. Nonsense! He is interested in your spirit and your body, which is the temple of the Holy Spirit. *(I Corinthians 6:19-20)*

Tell me, if the Holy Spirit is removed, how can anybody be saved? Jesus declared in *John 6:44, "No man can come to Me except the Father who sent me draw him... "* Tell me, if God's Spirit is removed, how can anyone be drawn? To compound their error, they tell us the natural Jew is going to do in 3½ to 7 years <u>without</u> the Holy Spirit what God has been doing for 2,000 years <u>with</u> the Holy Spirit working with the church. Does that make sense? Think it over. How long has our Heavenly Father been dealing with you? Can you imagine trying to live for God if He withdrew His Spirit? Impossible!

Years ago I believed the teaching of the "rapture." Sure, I was taught it at Bible College. I had Larkin's charts on futurism. As a matter of fact, I spent weeks making a large colored chart with the dragon with 7 heads, 10 horns, 10 crowns, the beast, false prophet and all the other weird details concerning the antichrist. Then I happened to read his exposition on the three frogs that come up out of the pit. He postulated that one of the frogs was the Pentecostal movement. I said to myself, "I've received the baptism of the Spirit. Surely if he is wrong about the precious experience of being immersed in the Holy Spirit, what else is he wrong about?" I folded my chart, walked to the burn barrel in the back of the house and burned it. I don't regret it one bit! To tell you the truth, I didn't get anywhere with God until I burned those false teachings. I ask you and plead with you, "Don't be beguiled by tradition, false teaching, or heap to yourself teachers having itching ears." These people may be sincere, but sincerity has never been the litmus test for truth. The highest form of worship is obedience. Sure, it will cost you something to jettison past teachings that are patently false.

The closer you walk with God, sometimes the more you walk alone. God's approval may cost you the disapproval of man, but better to have God's smile than man's smile.

Can You Walk Alone With the Lord?

You point out that Jesus had crowds. Sure, He had the loaves and fishes crowd – 5,000 men not counting women and children. But they left Him. So did some of His disciples. Jesus had some hard things to say. In *John 6:66* the Bible says, *"From that time many of His disciples went back and walked with Him no more."* Eating His flesh and drinking His blood was the issue. Do you realize they no longer walked with him? Where is your line of demarcation? How deep is your commitment? Will you go with Him through the garden? The disciples didn't – they ran. Will you go with Him through the judgment? Be careful, now. None of Jesus' disciples did. What about you? Our next topic is on being an overcomer. Is that a driving ambition, a goal of yours? Let's take the word "overcomer." What does it presuppose – some obstacle, hurdle, something to surmount, a trial, something to vanquish and subdue, to get the victory and maintain it? I'm sure your desire is to be an "overcomer."

Chapter 3

God's Promise – He Will Perfect His Word

Did you know that all the promises in the book of Revelation are given to OVERCOMERS? Following are a list of verses regarding OVERCOMING. Read them slowly. Read them carefully. Remember, these promises are only to OVERCOMERS.

1. *Revelation 2:7 – "He that hath an ear, let him hear what the Spirit saith unto the churches; To him that OVERCOMETH will I give to eat of the tree of life, which is in the midst of the paradise of God."*
2. *Revelation 2:11 – "He that hath an ear, let him hear what the Spirit saith unto the churches; He that OVERCOMETH shall not be hurt of the second death."*
3. *Revelation 2:17 – "He that hath an ear, let him hear what the Spirit saith unto the churches; To him that OVERCOMETH will I give to eat of the hidden manna, and will give him a white stone, and in the stone a new name written, which no man knoweth saving he that receiveth it."*
4. *Revelation 2:26-28 – "And he that OVERCOMETH and keepeth my works unto the end, to him will I give power over the nations: And he shall rule them with a rod of iron; as the vessels of a potter shall they be broken to shivers; even as I received of my Father. And I will give him the morning star."*
5. *Revelation 3:5 – "He that OVERCOMETH, the same shall be clothed in white raiment; and I will not blot out his name out of the book of life, but I will confess his name before my Father, and before His angels."*
6. *Revelation 3:12 – "Him that OVERCOMETH will I make a pillar in the temple of my God, and he shall go no more out: and I will write upon him the name of my God, and the name of the city of my God, which is new Jerusalem, which cometh down out of heaven from my God: and I will write upon him my new name."*
7. *Revelation 3:21 – "To him that OVERCOMETH will I grant to sit with me in my throne, even as I also OVERCAME, and am set down with my Father in his throne."*
8. *Revelation 12:10 – "And I heard a loud voice saying in heaven, Now is come salvation, and strength, and the kingdom of our God, and the power of His Christ: for the accuser of our brethren is cast down, which accused them before our God day and night."*
9. *Revelation 12:11 – "And they OVERCAME him by the blood of the Lamb, and by the word of their testimony; and they loved not their lives unto the death."*

10. *Revelation 17:14 – "These shall make war with the Lamb, and the Lamb shall OVERCOME them: for He is Lord of lords, and King of kings: and they that are with Him are called, and chosen, and faithful."*
11. *Revelation 21:7 – "He that OVERCOMETH shall inherit all things; and I will be his God, and he shall be My son.'*

Please look at that last verse we quoted. What are the OVERCOMERS going to inherit? All things! Can you believe, all things? It seems to me, there's the verse that directly speaks to us, the believers, right now – today, in *Matthew 6:33, "But seek ye first the kingdom of God (not the rapture) and His righteousness and ALL THESE THINGS* (emphasis added) *shall be added unto you."* By the way, where is this kingdom going to be? *Revelation 5:9-10* declares, *"Thou wast slain and hast redeemed us to God by Thy blood out of every kindred, and tongue, and people and nation;" Verse 10, "And hast made us unto our God a kingdom of priests and we shall reign ON THE EARTH."* (emphasis added)

Do you understand? What has been our Heavenly Father's ultimate intention? To understand we must go back to the very first chapter of the Bible. *Genesis 1:26* says, *"And God said, Let us make man in our image, after our likeness and let them have dominion over the fish of the sea and over the fowl of the air, and over the cattle and OVER ALL THE EARTH!!!* I think it is essential to understand that our God did not say, "Let us make the devil and let him have dominion," but that is what the prophecy experts try to tell us. But our God has designed that mankind is to exercise authority over His creation. God has never ever rescinded His command. Our task is to disciple nations and bring them under His influence and Biblical principles. God help us to develop a winning, aggressive attitude. Come on; let's stop running from the enemy. We've got it backwards. The enemy should be running from us!!

The Problem is a Complacent Church

Psalms 115:16 says, *"The heaven, even the heavens, are the Lord's, but the EARTH hath HE GIVEN to THE CHILDREN OF MEN."* (emphasis added). He didn't create the earth to give it to the antichrist and his crowd. If we believe the rapture theory, we somehow are placed in a twilight zone of benign neutrality. We will lose the concept of the church militant and become the church complacent. What is the result of that? By cunning deceit and our abdication of responsibility, we allow evil men to saddle us with sickening laws to further enslave our children and us – without a whimper of protest. Bible reading and prayer removed from schools. Who allowed it? We did – the silent majority. Roe vs. Wade. Who allowed it? We did – the silent majority. What is the result? Our public schools have become immoral swamps breeding mosquitoes of hate and government indoctrination centers, which are failing on a massive scale to teach our children basic skills of reading, writing and arithmetic.

When we adopt an evacuation theology and believe the devil's taking over the planet, it can't but show in statements like,

"You can't fight city hall" or "It's useless."

Does this sound like victory? We all end up with spiritual lockjaw, afraid to speak and afraid to be different. Like an old

> **Let's stop running from the enemy. We've got it backwards. The enemy should be running from us!!**

preacher said, "We're like arctic rivers, frozen at the mouth." But Jesus said in *Revelation 12:11, "And they overcame him (the devil) by the blood of the lamb, and by the word of their testimony and THEY LOVED NOT THEIR LIVES UNTO THE DEATH."* (emphasis added). Is there anything for which you are willing to die, anything for which you are willing to lay it on the line? My friend, the greatest love is not found in the bedroom. The greatest love is manifested on the battlefield. Jesus said in *John 15:13, "Greater love hath no man than this, that a man lay down his life for his friends."* Take a good look at Calvary (the battle for the souls of men). What is lovely about a broken form of a dying man with hot, sticky blood running down his body – a body so bruised and beaten with spit dripping from His beard where men spat on Him, plucked His beard, impaled on a torture stake. Yet He spoke these words, *"Father, forgive them for they know not what they do."* Ah, lovely Golgotha, wonderful Calvary. No wonder the song bursts from our heart:

"Redeemed, how I love to proclaim it,"
or "Love so amazing, so divine demands my soul, my life, my all."

Perfection Through Suffering

Jesus <u>overcame</u> death, hell and the grave. *I John 4:17* states, *"...because as He is, so are we in the world."* We are His body, the body of Christ. *Hebrews 2:9-10* says, *"But we see Jesus who was made a little lower than the angels for the <u>suffering</u> of death, crowned with glory and honor; that He, by the grace of God should taste death for every man."* Verse 10, *"For it became Him, for whom are all things, and by whom are all things, in bringing many sons to glory, to make the captain of their salvation perfect through <u>sufferings</u>."* You know what the bottom line is? No <u>sufferings</u>, no GLORY – plain and simple.

Do you know what is really amazing? You should thank God for the privilege of living in America, for freedom to worship God according to the dictates of your heart. Most Christians outside of the western world are persecuted, vilified, ostracized, and criticized for their faith. Many have laid down their lives and have gone through agonizing torture. Yet, we sit in air-conditioned, plush, cushioned pews, listening to sweet sermonettes that produce Christianettes. Of course, on Sunday we better be out no later than 12 o'clock Noon so we can beat the Methodists to our favorite restaurant. Shame on us! Where are the warriors, the battle tested veterans, the intercessors that will weep for our vitiated, paltry condition?

Dr. Billy Graham has said on different occasions that the 20th century has produced more martyrs than all the other centuries combined. Does that ever move you to get on your knees and pray mightily? Are we mesmerized by materialism? How long has it been that a prayer burden has caused you to have Jeremiah eyes – a fountain of tears? Yet, we shed glycerin tears over some Hollywood flick that is filled with immorality and profanity. My friend, I certainly am not masochistic and enjoy pain and suffering, but what is going to happen if there is no escape? No rapture? Are you prepared to go through suffering or whatever comes in the days ahead? Now, please believe me, I do not want to put a guilt trip or a spirit of fear on anyone, but would you look with me at *Romans 8:14-17*? Surely we desire to be led by the Spirit. It says in *Verse 14, "For as many as are led by the Spirit of God, they are the sons of God."* Isn't that wonderful? Let's go on. *Verse 15, "For ye have not received the spirit of bondage to fear; but ye have received the spirit of adoption, whereby we cry, Abba, Father." Verse 16, "The Spirit Himself beareth witness with our spirit, that we are the children of God."* Watch now as Paul tells the Roman Christians in the previous verses that we are not to fear. What does he conclude this wonderful truth of being heirs and joint-heirs with? *Verse 17, "And if children, then heirs; heirs of God, and joint-heirs with Him* (now the clincher) *if so be that we SUFFER with him, that we may also be GLORIFIED* (emphasis added) *together."* Let me list some other salient scriptures that you, dear reader, can look up on your own. *Acts 5:41; Acts 9:16; Hebrews 11:25; James 5:10; I Peter 5:10.*

You're in Good Company

I know that you know Jesus is your elder brother, but did you know or ever imagine the disciples were also your brothers? They are, just many generations removed. Think of it. Peter, your brother; James, your brother; and the others, your brethren. Many of you know that John the Beloved, the one who leaned on Jesus, the Apostle of love, was the only disciple at the cross. Jesus, from the cross, commissioned John to take care of Mary, his mother. Yes, John is also your brother. Do you know what he declared when he received the revelation of Jesus Christ? Look with me in

Revelation 1:9. He tells you he's your brother but along with that, he states he's your companion. My companion, you ask? Companion of what? Here, let me quote it. *Verse 9, "I, John, who also am your BROTHER, and COMPANION IN TRIBULATION* (emphasis added), *and in the kingdom and patience of Jesus Christ, was in the isle that is called Patmos, for the word of God, and for the testimony of Jesus Christ. "* John said he was not only your brother but also a companion in tribulation. Of course, the word tribulation is the same word in the Greek for the Great Tribulation spoken of in *Matthew 24:21, 29.* Do you get the implication? I'm sure you do. You see, church history tells us that Nero tried to boil John in oil but he wouldn't die, so he banished John to a barren rocky island in the Aegean Sea. The island had a hostile environment and was uninhabitable. However, that was where John the Beloved received his greatest revelation – the unveiling of the Mighty Christ!

The Last Word to the Church

Many people think the last message Jesus gave us was to evangelize, such as *Matthew 28:19-20* or *Mark 16:15* where He commanded us to, "Go ye." No! No! My friend, check out *Revelation, Chapters 2 and 3.* If you've got a red-letter edition of the scriptures, you'll find that the words of these two chapters are written in red. Go ahead, read them. The last message to the church is not, "Go Ye" but "Repent." A man or woman who calls for repentance has set themselves against the tide of a religious, "I'm o.k. – you're o.k." sentiment. By the way, would you like to hear what John, your brother and companion in tribulation, had to say about overcoming? Let's look at a couple of scriptures in his first Epistle.

I John 2:13, "I write unto you, fathers, because ye have known him that is from the beginning. I write unto you, young men, because ye have OVERCOME the wicked one. I write unto you, little children, because ye have known the Father. " (emphasis added).

I John 4:3-4, "And every spirit that confesseth not that Jesus Christ is come in the flesh is not of God: and this is that spirit of antichrist, whereof ye have heard that it should come; and even now already is it in the world. " Verse 4, "Ye are of God, little children, and have OVERCOME (emphasis added). *them: because greater is He that is in you, than he that is in the world. "*

Do you realize what *Verse 3* is saying? The spirit of antichrist was in the world in John's day. John makes that very clear. Then he declares that we are of God because we confess that Jesus Christ is come in the flesh. Hallelujah! He then tells us in *Verse 4* that we have overcome those antichrist spirits, *"for GREATER is He that is in us than he that is in the*

21

world." Dear reader, that doesn't sound like the "rapture" to me. Does it sound like that to you?

I John 5:4-5, "For whatsoever is born of God <u>OVERCOMETH</u> the world: and this is the victory that <u>OVERCOMETH</u> the world, even our faith." Verse 5, "Who is he that <u>OVERCOMETH</u> the world, but he that believeth that Jesus Christ is the Son of God?"(emphasis added).

It seems the Holy Spirit that authored the words John wrote, believes more about our overcoming faith than we do. Please read these verses out loud to yourself and contemplate their majestic meaning and significance. On a personal note, *Verses 4-8* of *I John 5* turned my life upside down or rather, right side up in 1971.

In *I John 5:14-15*, His Word says, *"This is the confidence that we have in Him, that, if we ask any thing according to His will, He heareth us: and if we know that He heareth us, whatsoever we ask, we know that we have the petitions that we desired of Him."*

Because His word is true, as we conclude this part on overcoming, let me pray with you to:

1. Find God's will;

2. Come into agreement with God's will;

3. Speak God's will in prayer;

4. Review answers to prayer;

5. Declare scriptures out loud;

6. Fill your mouth with thanksgiving and praise; and

7. One final word – OBEY!!

Chapter 4

Man's Perversity – A Fabrication Of Deception – A Challenge

A major question to contemplate – who preached the message of the "rapture" before 1830? I'm talking about the year 1830 A.D. Can you believe that for 1800 years there was no teaching on the "rapture." I remind you again the word "rapture" is not to be found in your Bible. (I'll share with you later in this chapter the history of what happened in 1830.) I'm sure a great number of people from historic denominations have read Tim LaHaye's series of "Left Behind" books. They have sold like hot cakes. Who's buying them? Why, millions of people. Men and women, saved and unsaved, are interested in what's going to happen in the future. There has to be a hunger for spiritual understanding. Various Christian news services have said the "Left Behind" fiction book is at the top of the best-seller lists.

So, therefore, Lutherans, Presbyterians, Methodists, Baptist, Pentecostals, independents and dependents, stay-inners and come-outers, all have a fascination with what's going to happen at the Second Coming. And here is where I make my offer. If anyone can find where any of the early church fathers in the formation of the church taught the "rapture," any of the early church councils who taught the "rapture," any of the Godly men who figured in the Reformation who taught the "rapture," any of the Puritans who founded this great land of America who taught the "rapture," I will personally give you $1,000. You can't find any!! They never considered it nor wrote about it.

For the Lutherans that might read this book, consider Martin Luther who brought to us "Sola scripture" (only the scriptures) sola fide (by faith alone) and nailed his 95 point Thesis to the church door at Wittenburg, taking a stand against the largest religious system of his day, echoing those famous words, "I can do nothing else; here I stand." For his stand, he was ex-communicated by papal decree. What did he do? He wrote back to Rome and ex-communicated the Pope from the true Church. He was a brave man. Lutherans, listen to me, in all of his writings – not one word about any so-called "rapture." He wrote a lot but, sorry, no writing about a "rapture." What about Wycliff? Sorry, no writing about a "rapture."

John Calvin was a brilliant scholar and did more for furthering the Gospel with his "Biblical Institutes" by sharing with the world uneclipsed dogma in soteriology and predestination. Surely in the tomes that he penned, there must have been the teaching of the "rapture." Presbyterians and Baptists, Evangelical Free Churches – find me his teaching of the "rapture" (the going of the church). You won't find any such treatise! He believed in the dominion mandate – the Word of God applicable in every arena of life. What a Godly legacy he left our world. Simply stated, the teaching of the "rapture" is not to be found in his writings.

John and Charles Welsey, founders of the Methodist societies, never wanted to leave the Anglican Church. England was in deep political trouble and spiritual dearth. The country lay in the shadow of the French Revolution. Then at Epworth and Aldersgate, Wesley's heart was "strangely warmed" within him and he, his brother Charles, and George Whitfield set the British Isles ablaze with the power of the Gospel through the doctrine of sanctification and holy living. Not only in England but also in their many trips to the colonies, they caused a great stirring and revival wherever they preached. Did they preach the "rapture?" No! Try to find it in their writings and their preachments. Sorry, it isn't there; it is non-existent! Men and women from Georgia to New England were won to Christ through godly, solid scriptural exposition but again; they held no prophecy conferences on the "rapture."

A Brief History

So, you say, "What happened in 1830?" Well, let me quote from the late Bill Britton, who writes about Edward Irving and Margaret McDonald. I quote, "Perhaps you have heard of the Irvingite movement known as the Catholic Apostolic church. The Encyclopedia Brittanica, 1966 issue, Vol. 12, pages 648-649 describes Edward Irving and the controversy over his teachings in Scotland and England in the early 1800's. He was excommunicated by the London Presbytery, and in 1833 was condemned and deposed from the ministry of the Church of Scotland because of his teaching concerning "the sinfulness of Christ's humanity." He also began to teach a "rapture of the church" after a young Scottish lass by the name of Margaret McDonald went into a trance and described a vision in which she said she saw the saints leaving the earth at the return of the Lord, before the "tribulation." Her "revelation" was recommended in a book written by R. N. Norton and printed in London in 1861. Prior to this time, the church, all the way back to the Apostles, had always preached that the church would go victoriously through the tribulation. There is no record of the "escape rapture" theory being preached before 1830. On April 30, 1831, a Mrs. J. B. Cardale, who later joined Irving's church, had uttered a personal revelation of a "pre-tribulation rapture."

It was from this supposed revelation that the modern doctrine and modern phraseology respecting it arose. It came not from scripture but from that which falsely pretended to be the Spirit of God. Edward Irving accepted this teaching and it was taught at prophetic meetings at Powers Courthouse in

Ireland, attended much by Plymouth Brethren organizer, John Darby. Irving's views influenced Darby, C. H. Mackintosh, and C. I. Scofield (whose Bible notes popularized the new theory). So, it was a young Scottish girl who originated this idea, and is so recorded on page 15 of Norton's book on the Catholic Apostolic church. Darby and Scofield, along with Clarence Larkin and his charts, began to teach this new theory. In the early 1900's, it reached a peak in popularity." (end of Bill Britton quote).

There are several books that deal extensively with the Irvingite, Millerite and "rapture" theory movement. It is not my intention to probe further into the erroneous and spurious. Let's move on in our desire to inquire further of who's staying and who's leaving. First, we'll start with Old Testament scriptures and then move into the New Testament and finally try to see what *I Thessalonians 4:16-18* says. This is the sole and primary scripture the futurists choose to quote. When the Word declares in *II Peter 1:20*, *"Knowing this first, that no prophecy of the scripture is of any private interpretation."* What this means is a student of the Word of God cannot take one scripture and make a doctrine out of it. You cannot take one verse and assassinate or void another verse of scripture. There has to be a harmony of the flow of truth. That's why *"at the mouth of 2 or 3 witnesses let every matter be established."* References are: *Deuteronomy 17:6, Deuteronomy 19:15, Matthew 18:16, I Corinthians 13:1, I Timothy 5:19.* Two or three witnesses are essential to build a doctrine that has a strong foundation. That's why we don't baptize for the dead like the Mormons do. It is only alluded to once in scripture and that is in *I Corinthians 15:29.* You simply cannot build a Biblical truth on just one verse. That being established, let's move on.

Chapter 5

Man's Perplexity – We Have It Backwards

"OK," you say, "What does the Old Testament have to say about leaving and staying?" First, let's go to *Psalms 37:9, "For evildoers shall be cut off: but those who wait upon the Lord shall inherit* "heaven" NO *"the earth."* Tell me according to this verse, who is cut off? The answer is: the evildoers.

Psalms 37:11, "But the meek shall inherit the earth; and shall delight themselves in the abundance of peace." Who's staying here? The meek!!! What are they inheriting? The earth!!

Psalms 37:18, 20, "The Lord knoweth the days of the upright; and their inheritance shall be forever." Verse 20, *"But the wicked shall perish, and the enemies of the Lord shall be like the fat of lambs: they shall consume; into smoke shall they consume away."* In these two verses, who's staying – the upright! Who's leaving – the wicked are consumed.

Psalms 37:28-29, "For the Lord loveth judgment and forsaketh not His saints; they are preserved forever: but the seed of the wicked shall be cut off." Verse 29, *"The righteous shall inherit the land and dwell therein forever."* I know I keep asking the same question but in *Verse 28*, who leaves, who gets cut off? The wicked. Who stays and inherits the earth, the land? The righteous.

Psalms 37:34-38, "Wait on the Lord, and keep His way, and He shall exalt thee to inherit the land: when the wicked are cut off, thou shalt see it." Verse 35, *"I have seen the wicked in great power, and spreading himself like a green bay tree."* Verse 36, *"Yet he passed away, and lo, he was not: yea, I sought him, but he could not be found."* Verse 37, *"Mark the perfect man, and behold the upright: for the end of that man is peace."* Verse 38, *"But the transgressors shall be destroyed together: the end of the wicked shall be cut off."* OK, one final time in this 37th *Psalm*, who is cut off? Who is in great power? Who passed away? Who are destroyed together? Who leave? The wicked! Who inherits the land? Who has peace? Who is staying? THE UPRIGHT!!

Let's turn to the book of *Proverbs* written by one of the wisest men of all times. Can Solomon shed any light on who's leaving and who's staying? Well, let's see. Turn to *Proverbs 2:21-22, "For the upright shall dwell in the land, and the perfect shall remain in it."* Verse 22, *"But the wicked shall be cut off from the earth, and the transgressors shall be rooted out of it."* Who does Solomon say remains and dwells in the land? It is very clear.

The upright and the perfect! Who does he say gets cut off and rooted out (raptured out)? The wicked and transgressors!

How about *Proverbs 10:29-30, "The way of the Lord is strength to the upright: but destruction shall be to the workers of iniquity." Verse 30, "The righteous shall NEVER BE REMOVED: but the wicked shall not inhabit the earth."* (emphasis added). My, oh my, that's very clear! Who <u>never</u> gets removed? The upright and righteous! Who leaves? Again, it's the wicked!

> **"The crying need of the present day church is "Holy Ghost baptized brains."**

Seeing that these scriptures declare that the wicked are removed, an inquiring person will usually sit back, ponder, think and then ask themselves, "Well, what about what the Bible says about, "one shall be taken and the other left?" Doesn't *Matthew 24* have a lot to say about that?" Yes, it does and when Jesus began explaining the events that were going to take place, the first thing He said was, *"Take heed, that no man deceive you."* Have you ever been deceived? Why sure! But during the time you were deceived, were you aware of it? Probably not. The application of God's Word in our lives is the antidote for deception.

Well, when we examine scripture, let's begin with the insight and instruction of Jesus, *"do not be deceived."* Follow the law of Bible interpretation: (1) Let scripture interpret scripture (the Bible is the best commentary on itself); (2) Follow the harmony of the context (a text without a context is a pretext); and (3) Spiritual things are spiritually discerned (the Holy Spirit is the best interpreter of the Book that He moved upon men to write).

So right now turn to *Matthew 24.* Read the context leading up to *Verse 34,* letting scripture interpret scripture. Praying for the Holy Spirit's guidance and knowing that the Word and the Spirit always agree, look at *Verses 35-36, "Heaven and earth shall pass away, but My Words shall not pass away. But of that day and hour knoweth no man, no, not the angels of heaven, but My Father only."* Hold on, right here. Most people interpret this as the second coming. I will make my position clear on this in a closing chapter; however, for right now, go ahead and read it again. What does the previous verse say? Heaven and earth are going to pass away! Of <u>that day</u> knoweth no man. What day? The <u>day</u> that heaven and earth pass away! What's the important emphasis here? His Word will never pass away! Become part of the Word, part of the permanent, not the passing – His Word in you, you in His Word. Didn't Jesus say that He was the light of the world *(John 8:12)* and didn't He turn to His disciples and tell them in

Matthew 5:14, "Ye are the light of the world." Don't we sing that children's song, "This little light of mine, I'm going to let it shine." Don't the scriptures say?

In *Romans 13:12, "...to put on the armor of light."*

In *II Corinthians 4:6, "God commanded the light to shine in our hearts."*

In *Ephesians 5:8, "...ye are light, walk as children of light."*

In *I Peter 2:9, "We are called out of darkness into His marvelous light."*

In *James 1:17, "Every perfect gift...comes from the Father of lights..."*

Getting Rid of False Teaching

If the day of Pentecost was the birthday of the church *(Acts, Chapter 2)* and it was, do you recall what observable, physical phenomena was associated with the 120 that were filled with the Holy Spirit? First of all, what does the Bible say about your spirit? *Proverbs 20:27* declares, *"The spirit of man is the candle* (lamp) *of the Lord, searching all the inward parts."* So...? On the day of Pentecost there were seen on the disciples and the believers CLOVEN TONGUES OF FIRE! Hallelujah! The Heavenly lamplighter has come to light your mind, burn out the dross (false doctrine and tradition), remove darkness (ignorance), banish fear and give you the power of love and a sound mind. As a friend of mine, George Southwick, once said, "The crying need of the present day church is "Holy Ghost-baptized brains." A marvelous purpose of the Holy Spirit's coming is found in *John 14:26, "But the Comforter, who is the Holy Spirit, whom the Father will send in my Name, He shall teach you all things and bring all things to your remembrance, whatsoever I have said unto you."* With the full assurance and the promise of the Spirit's sure guidance, let's look for truth with a hunger at what was happening in Noah's day.

In Noah's day, who was "taken" and who was "left?" Wicked taken, righteous left.

In Noah's day, did he and his family go THROUGH the flood of judgment? Yes.

Were they preserved? Yes.

Did they go through the tribulation of that day? Yes.

Did God destroy the earth (I mean terra firma)? No.

Next question: Did God destroy the world? Which world – the world of soil, trees, vegetation? No! Well, I'm sure it was devastated but eventually it grew back. How about the world of wicked men? Yes! How about the world of violence that filled the earth? Yes, that world was destroyed. How about the world of politics of Noah's day? Yes! That world was destroyed.

Now having at least questioned and considered a few of the "worlds" that were destroyed, let's read the text from *Matthew* that speaks about the flood. *Matthew 24:37-41, "But as the days of Noah were, so shall also the coming of the Son of man be. Verse 38, For as in the days that were before the flood they were eating and drinking, marrying and giving in marriage, until the day that Noah entered into the ark." Verse 39, "And knew not UNTIL THE FLOOD CAME AND TOOK THEM ALL AWAY; SO SHALL ALSO THE COMING (emphasis added) of the Son of man be," Verse 40, "Then two shall be in the field, the one shall be taken, and the other left." Verse 41, "Two women shall be grinding at the mill; the one shall be taken, and the other left."*

Pastors, evangelists, and popular teachers of our day use the last two verses of *"two shall be in the field, one taken and one left"* and *"two women shall be grinding, one taken and one left,"* to prove that the righteous are leaving, to prove the "rapture" theory. My dear friend, please remember the context – *"In Noah's day."* That phrase is very important! As a matter of fact, that is the subject, so we must apply the principles of accurate Biblical interpretation along with intellectual honesty. Accordingly, may I ask, "Who is leaving and who is staying?" Shocked? I was! Why, it's exactly the opposite of what I had been taught. How about you?

Speaking of being shocked, let me ask you another question. What kind of therapy has been utilized in the past in psychoanalysis to break a pattern of bad thinking? Hasn't it been "shock therapy?" What do you think the Holy Spirit is? Fire and power – the power of God is given to shock you. The ministry of the Spirit's job is to break up thought patterns that are false and harmful to you. So if you view these scriptures in an unbiased new light and you're shocked, you can praise God that the Spirit is at work in your life. If you need to take time to read and re-read the text, go ahead before we proceed. I desire Biblical, honest, sound and sane knowledge. Do you? How do we acquire this knowledge? Do you know how it comes? Little by little – that's how! Look at what *Isaiah 28:9-10* says, *"Whom shall He teach knowledge? And whom shall He make to understand doctrine: Those who are weaned from the milk and drawn from the breasts." Verse 10, "Precept must be upon precept, line upon line, line upon line, here a little and there a little."*

You may think this next paragraph is little and insignificant, but I consider it big. Let me explain. One of the largest Pentecostal denominations, The Assemblies of God, would probably be considered to be futuristic in their eschatology; however, years ago an article was printed in the official publication of the Assemblies of God – the "Pentecostal Evangel." That particular issue is dated January 1, 1967, "Official Voice of the Assemblies of God," Springfield, Missouri. On page 9 of the Evangel, in an article about the *24th Chapter of Matthew*, we read, and I quote, "Contrary to what is often taught, the rapture is NOT (emphasis added) in evidence here. Those "taken" are the wicked, who are taken in judgment – just as the wicked in Noah's time (mentioned in the preceding verse) were taken in judgment. Those "left" are the righteous who remain to enjoy the blessings of the Millennium which will follow Christ's return to earth" (end of quote).

Now I am aware this was written years ago, and I don't know if there has been a change of doctrinal position or not. Nonetheless, they, at that time were willing to state in their official publication that those verses quoted did not pertain to the "rapture" but indicated the removal of the wicked. Those of you in that denomination perhaps could inquire further to see if they still stand by that interpretation today.

Before we explain *I Thessalonians 4:15-17* from another point of view other than the usual futuristic slant, let's for a moment consider the structure of the parables of *Matthew 13*. Do the teachings of Jesus indicate to you and me anything concerning the end of the age? Why did Jesus do most of His teaching using parables? Let *Matthew* tell us plainly.

Matthew 13:10-11, 16-17, "And the disciples came, and said unto Him, "Why speakest Thou to them in parables?" Verse 11, "He answered and said unto them, "Because it is given unto you to know the mysteries of the Kingdom of heaven, but to them it is not given." Verse 16," But blessed are your eyes for they see: and your ears, for they hear." Verse 17, "For verily I say unto you, that many prophets and righteous men have desired to see those things which ye see and have not seen them; and to hear those things which ye hear and have not heard them."

The parables were spoken for two reasons: (1) to conceal, and (2) to reveal. When the scriptures declare, *"Ye shall know the truth and the truth shall make you free"* in *John 8:32*, what does it make you free from? From ignorance. Aren't you concerned with some of the juvenile and sophomoric attitudes that prevail among those that name the name of Christ? Our people suffer because of profound ignorance, not only among themselves but also on the part of their leadership. At a recent prestigious pastors' conference, the high dollar promoters were addressing the conferees and telling them not to teach people they are "sinners" but that they are just "pre-saved." They were admonished further to implement "user-friendly" religion. This shows either the height of ignorance or an all time low in maturity, or a lack of courage – or all three.

The Truth Hurts

Today, it seems the way to get a crowd is to water down the message and not offend anyone. Truth can be downright offensive. As a matter of fact in our day, the way to empty out a church is not to preach false doctrine. The way to empty it, is to teach <u>truth</u>!

Hosea 4:6 declares, *"My people are destroyed for lack of knowledge."* *Jeremiah 12:10* says, *"Many pastors have destroyed my vineyard."* Jeremiah goes on to say in *Jeremiah 50:6, "My people have been lost sheep:their shepherds have caused them to go astray."* What an indictment! When you gain truth, you also gain responsibility and accountability. The more knowledge you have, the more power you have. Do you want power? Then gain knowledge by rejecting tradition and applying the principles of the sword of the Spirit. It is sharp, it will cut, and it will divide. Divide what? Truth from error, fact from fiction, and reality from religious rhetoric.

With that said, let's look at *Matthew 13:24-30, "Another parable put He forth unto them saying, the Kingdom of heaven is likened unto a man who sowed good seed in his field: Verse 25, "But while men slept, his enemy came and sowed tares among the wheat, and went his way." Verse 26, "But when the blade was sprung up, and brought forth fruit, then appeared the tares also." Verse 27, So the servants of the house holder came and said unto him, "Sir didst thou not sow good seed in thy field? From whence then hath it tares?" Verse 28, "He said unto them, An enemy hath done this. The servants said unto him, Wilt thou then that we go and gather them up?" Verse 29, "But he said, Nay; lest while ye gather up the tares, ye root up also the wheat with them." Verse 30, "Let both grow together until the harvest: and in the time of the harvest I will say to the reapers, "Gather ye together FIRST (emphasis added) the tares, and bind them in bundles to burn them: but gather the wheat into my barn."*

Did you get that last verse? Who is bundled first? The <u>WICKED</u> – the <u>TARES</u> – the <u>UNRIGHTEOUS</u>! Jesus said, *"gather together FIRST* (emphasis added) *the tares."* He didn't say, gather the righteous and have them fly away. No! No! The tares, my friend, get bundled and removed. What happens when the tares get bundled? Let's continue and find out.

Bundled for the Burning

Have you ever considered what the bundles are? Aren't the wicked joining together in political action committees to further their agendas against morals and Christian values? Aren't there coalitions that gather together (*"bundle"*) to promote wickedness such as Queer Nation, the A.D.L. and various anti-Biblical, ultra-liberal feminist organizations? Why are they joining league with one another? Why does the pro-abortion movement seek approval from the bodies of Planned Parenthood and the A.M.A.? I tell you, they are being bundled together for removal. The scriptures in this parable are abundantly clear. They are first to leave! That's precisely why I want to stay! Let me stay to inherit the Kingdom prepared from the foundation of the world.

After Jesus had spoken the above parable concerning the wheat and the tares, the disciples didn't understand it. So they questioned Him and asked Him to elucidate and explain it to them in terms they could comprehend. You see, they didn't fathom what He was saying. Many times I have felt the same way, asking, "Lord, I need further explanation. Won't you help me?"

One of the first things Jesus did was recorded in *Matthew 13:36, "Then Jesus sent the multitude away."* Sometimes, no, perhaps most of the time, Jesus sends the multitude away for they are not interested in probing and finding deep truths that are hidden to the casual seeker. After all, didn't He say in *Matthew 7:7, "Ask, and ye shall receive; seek, and ye shall find; knock and the door will be opened to you."* You may question, "Well, how do I seek after truth?" First, know this: Truth is not a philosophy, a creed or a standardized summation of Biblical facts. Truth is a person – the person of Christ. Seek Him. Jeremiah told us in *Jeremiah 29:13, "And ye shall see ME, and find ME, when ye shall search for ME with ALL* (emphasis added) *your heart."* The multitude that day must have been casual followers because Jesus sent them away. But to the hungry and thirsty, He waits for the appointed time, to satisfy the hungry with good things. *(Luke 1:53)*

So they asked Him in *Matthew 13:36, "Declare unto us the parable of the tares of the field."* Please notice the simple yet succinct explanation. Jesus explains this parable precept upon precept, line upon line, and tells them explicitly so that the truth would be unmistakably clear. *Verse 37, "He answered and said unto them, "He that sowed the good seed is the Son of man."* (Got it? Jesus has planted the good seeds). Then *Verse 38, "The field is the world"* (why, sure, that's plain enough). Go on, *"the good seed are the children of the Kingdom"* (that's you, dear reader). Go on, *"but the tares are the children of the wicked one"* (sure, that's the children of the enemy). *Verse 39, "The enemy that sowed them is the devil"* (it can't get any plainer than that). Let's go on, *"the harvest is the end of the age"* (Ok, so now we have a time frame). Let's proceed, *"and the reapers are the angels."*

The next verse, *Verse 40,* begins with, *"As therefore"* meaning – He is bringing the aforementioned statements to a conclusion. Let's follow these facts to a Biblical conclusion. *Verse 40, "As therefore, the tares are gathered and burned in the fire,* (watch this, now) *so shall it be in the end of this age.* (The King James Version has the word "world" for age and the Greek word is "aion" which is better translated "age.") When Jesus says, *"So shall it be at the end of this* (world) *age,"* you must go back to *Verse 30,* which says, *"Let both* (good seed and bad seed) *grow together until the harvest and in the time of harvest I will say to the reapers "Gather together FIRST the tares."*

Jesus our Savior, Redeemer and King, the One who authored the Bible, said, *"Gather FIRST the tares."* I'll tell you what: before any Bible thumping futuristic preacher or wannabe theologian that says the good seed, the wheat, are going first, I'll believe Jesus. He said the tares are leaving first! Who are you going to believe? Some popular preacher? Some noted Bible teacher? Some popular book? Fictitious literature? or Jesus? Why wouldn't you, out of all the above, choose Jesus' words?

Well, let's finish reading what Jesus said in *Verse 41, "The Son of man shall send forth His angels and they shall gather OUT* (emphasis added) *of His Kingdom all things that offend and them who do iniquity."*

Again I ask, "Who gets raptured out?" My friend, it's the wicked, the offensive and those that commit iniquity. I then have to ask why do the popular denominational leaders who say they love God's Word commit so great an error as to say "the righteous leave and the wicked antichrist is going to rule the world. Not so! Jesus ends the explanation of the parable by first disposing of the wicked and then declaring in *Verse 43, "Then* (when? ...after the tares have been removed first) *then shall the righteous* (the good seed) *shine forth as the sun in the Kingdom of their Father." "Who has ears to hear let him hear."*

My friend, are you hearing what the Holy Spirit is saying, or are you hearing what the denomination is saying, or are you hearing what you want to hear?

You might now say, "Well, how could so many well meaning, sincere people be wrong? Why, what you're saying is opposed to what I've been taught for years? How could all these people be in error?"

I have no theological ax to grind. I like to have friends, to be well liked and be popular. But this is not popular teaching and Bible exposition. God has not called us to a popularity contest. Only to stand for truth, not with warlike belligerence and not with haughtiness, arrogance or pride, but to be clothed with humility, being faithful to share with God's people so they may prepare for what lies ahead.

A Personal Example

Nearly 20 years ago, an evangelical Presbyterian pastor gathered with a group of pastors and Christian businessmen that met every Thursday morning at a local restaurant for prayer and fellowship. We had a separate dining area where we would have a light breakfast, sing choruses and pray for each other and our ministries. This particular group of men did this for years and was a great source of blessing and inspiration to me. This godly Presbyterian pastor felt a call to the mission field working with Brother Andrew, who wrote the book "God's Smuggler." His ministry was smuggling Bibles behind the "iron curtain" and the 'bamboo curtain." China and Russia were two of the countries to which he was sent. About a year later he returned. The fire had been kindled in his heart. He was a man with a mission. I mean you could tell it – his eyes sparkled and glistened both with fire and tears at the reports of victory and sorrow at what he experienced.

He stunned a lot of preachers that day. I'll never forget it, and I'll never forget what he said concerning the suffering church in China.

He first prefaced what he was going to say by declaring, "I know many of you will not want to hear what I have to report" and that probably whet our appetite even more. He proceeded to tell us, "I've been to China many times and these precious persecuted saints with tears flowing down their cheeks thanked us for the Bibles we brought and told us, please bring more Bibles, more of the Word of God written in our language." Hesitating for a moment he went on to drop a verbal hand grenade in the minds of quite a few men that morning when he said, "but I've got to tell you this also: the leaders of the underground church said they didn't want American missionaries to come and preach the "foolish doctrine of the rapture." For many of the Chinese Christians did not expect to have to give their lives during the "great purge" by the Communist insurgency." He said while being tortured those saints were crying for the "rapture" during their martyrdom. It was very quiet that Thursday morning, very sobering, serious and shocking to many. What makes us better than those Chinese Christians? Don't you think they felt like they were going through "the great tribulation?"

More recently Pastor Nelson Price, retired minister of Roswell Street Baptist Church in Marietta, Georgia, was preaching on the radio. His pastorate numbers in the 8,000 to 10,000 range. While preaching on courage in the face of persecution, he mentioned the story of Watchman Nee. Many of you have read or heard of his many books. Probably his most recognized and popular book is "The Normal Christian Life" which in our day is not "normal."

He went on to say that the Communists captured Watchman Nee and in the village square in front of many of his fellow Christians, the Communists asked him to recant and to deny Christ, which he would not. They informed the crowd that their pastor Watchman Nee would never write another book, and with one swift swipe of a sword they cut off his hands.

He could be heard thanking and praising God for the books that had been written and that he was able to suffer for his Savior. They silenced him that day, but he being dead yet speaketh – through his books and unswerving loyalty to the King of Kings. There was no rapture for Watchman Nee.

We may not be asked or required to die a martyr's death, but to believe a false teaching such as "an any moment rapture" is to belittle the sacrifice by those who have given their all. Read "Foxes Book of Martyrs" or "Jesus Freaks" by DC Talk and "Voice of the Martyrs" found at your local Christian bookstore.

Now let's proceed to the verses in *I. Thessalonians 4:15-18* and try to exegete and delineate this passage perhaps in a perspective you have not considered or perhaps you've never entertained. Let's read it together. *Verse 15, "For this we say unto you by the Word of the Lord that we who are alive and <u>REMAIN</u> (emphasis added) unto the coming of the Lord* (not the going of the saints) *shall not prevent (precede) them who are asleep." Verse 16, "For the Lord Himself shall descend from heaven with a SHOUT with the voice of an archangel and with the TRUMP of God and the dead in Christ shall rise first." Verse 17, "Then we who are alive and REMAIN (emphasis added) shall be caught up together with them in the clouds to meet the Lord in the air and so shall we ever be with the Lord." Verse 18, "Wherefore so comfort one another with these words."*

You may ask, "OK, what are you trying to prove? Just because you emphasized the word 'REMAIN' doesn't change the verse's meaning." But the word REMAIN isn't the word I really want to point out. What if I were to point out <u>three</u> significant words such as 'SHOUT', 'TRUMPET' and 'CAUGHT UP' and found them throughout your Bible? Would you be interested enough to investigate to see if the language of *I Thessalonians Chapter 4 verses 15-18* was found in other portions of scripture? What if those passages showed the cry of *I Thessalonians 4:15-18* is not a call to leave and evacuate but rather a battle cry to fight and conquer? What if you find the passage is about victory and resurrection power?

Please go with me on a fascinating journey through the Old Testament and New Testament and let's apply the principles of "search and find." Let's do it reasonably, rationally and practically. Remember we are searching for the words: (1) Shout, (2) Trumpet, and (3) Caught up. Let me ask one more time: "If you see Truth, are you willing to change?" Are you desirous to adjust your sights and perspective? Let's ask the Holy Spirit to do what He does best – lead us and guide us into all truth!

Chapter 6

Moses The Lawgiver – Caught Up In God

Moses and the Children of Israel (*Exodus, Chapter 19*)

Israel, God's covenant people, had just had a marvelous deliverance from a land of bondage and servitude, which was Egypt (a type of the flesh). They were delivered by the blood of the Lamb (their Passover). *Chapter 19* really is a chapter about Pentecost, for 50 days after they left Egypt (bondage of the flesh) they came to Mt. Sinai where Yahweh married them and the people became His national wife. We have Yahweh as the husband, God's covenant people as His wife, Moses as the officiator and the marriage certificate is the Ten Commandments.

Let me mention here that the whole nation was Pentecostal and were to observe the feast of Pentecost perpetually. I find it very interesting that this feast was held in the wilderness (which represents the testings of the soul, the mind). Passover was observed in Egypt to deliver them from the bondage of fleshly appetites (to which, sad to say, most of them longed to return). Pentecost was observed in the wilderness wanderings for 40 years. Don't you find it interesting that *I Corinthians 10:2* says, *"They were all baptized unto Moses in the <u>cloud</u> and in the <u>sea</u>?"* Of course that represented their water baptism "in the sea" where their enemies were drowned, and the cloud represented their "Holy Spirit" baptism, which led them for 40 years.

> **"Greater is He that is in you than he that is in the world."**

There is yet another feast to observe. The Feast of Tabernacles to be kept in the land of their inheritance. Isn't it marvelous to know that Pentecost is a down payment and that in Tabernacles there is more to come? Glory! The word, "Pentecost" in the Hebrew language simply means the number 50. If you desire to be a 100-fold Christian, then being "Pentecostal" means you're no more than half way there. Our Father has so much more for us. Let's sum this up giving you an abbreviated background for God's purposes:

1. Egypt: Passover celebrated - deliverance from the flesh

2. Wilderness: Pentecost celebrated - deliverance from your soul-mind, the real battleground

3. Canaan: Tabernacles celebrated - land of the fullness of the Spirit

Now before we proceed I know that it's popular to picture "Canaan's fair land as heaven," but it is simply not the truth, for Canaan is occupied by seven (7) nations. You've got to develop like David, the shepherd boy did and be a giant-killer. Don't "fly away, oh glory." Be like David. He was a man moving toward the enemy, not away from him! No beautiful isle of somewhere for David!

Possessing Your Possessions

Let's read from *Deuteronomy 7:1*. It begins with 'when', not 'if': *"When the Lord thy God shall bring thee into the land where thou goest to possess it* (Canaan) *and hath cast out many nations before thee, the Hittites, and the Girgashites and the Amorites and the Canaanites and the Perizzites and the Hivites and the Jebusites, seven* (7) *nations greater and mightier than thou."* Notice He says *"greater and mightier than thou"* but our God doesn't say, "greater and mightier than ME." The forces of antichrist and the powers of darkness are greater and mightier than 'you' in the natural, but remember *"Greater is He that is in you than he that is in the world."* *"Christ in you"* is a force that the world has yet to reckon with!

Now that we have a little background concerning *Exodus 19*. Let's proceed and see if we can find SHOUT, TRUMPET and CAUGHT UP. We don't go very far in the text for *Verse 3* says, *"And Moses went up unto God."* My first observation and question to you dear reader is, "Did Moses leave the planet?" No! Then where was he? The previous verse tells us that Israel was camped before the mount. Moses went up into the mountain and God was there. Moses never <u>left</u> the earth! The wonderful truth is: God can manifest Himself to you on the earth.

Now look with me to *Verses 5-6, "Now therefore, <u>if</u>* (conditional) *ye will obey my voice indeed and keep my covenant then ye shall be a peculiar treasure unto me above all people, for all the earth is mine." Verse 6, "And ye shall be unto Me a Kingdom of priests, and a holy nation. These are the words which thou shalt speak unto the children of Israel."*

You might at this point say, "Oh, well, that's the Old Testament" but, hold on, wait a minute. *Peter* in the first book that bears his name writes in *Chapter 2, Verse 9, "But ye are a chosen generation, a royal priesthood, a holy nation, a peculiar people, that ye should show forth the praises of Him who hath called you out of darkness into His marvelous light."*

Peter is quoting the *5th* and *6th verses* out of *Exodus 19*. Peter is reminding us that we are the people of the Book. We are in covenant with the Holy One of Israel, we bear the marks of God's Kingdom people, and we have been called out of darkness. What does darkness symbolize? Ignorance!

He's telling us to move into light – marvelous light, at that! Well, what's light? Truth!! *Psalms 119:105, "Thy Word is a lamp unto my feet and a light* (truth) *unto my path." Isaiah 60:1-2, "Arise, shine for thy light is come and the glory of the Lord is risen upon thee." Verse 2, "for, behold the darkness* (ignorance) *shall cover the earth and gross darkness* (great ignorance) *the people but the Lord shall arise upon thee and His glory shall be seen upon thee."* Revelation (God knowledge) is being revealed in this hour. Our national blindness is being removed! Praise Him!

Let's go back to *Exodus 19:9, "And the Lord said unto Moses, lo I come unto thee* (where?) *on the earth,* (how?) *in a thick cloud,* (why?) *that the people may hear when I speak with thee and believe thee forever."*

Now *Verse 11, "And be ready on the third day* (be ready, why?) *for the third day the Lord will COME DOWN* (emphasis added*) in the sight of all the people upon Mt Sinai."* I emphasize 'come down', because *I Thessalonians 4:16* starts with, *"For the Lord Himself shall descend* (come down) *from heaven."* Do you see the correlation here in Exodus? *"The Lord will COME DOWN."* "Well," you say, "where's the Shout, Trumpet, Caught up language?"

Hold on. We're coming to it in *Exodus 19:10*. The Lord told Moses to tell the people to sanctify themselves and purify themselves and to be ready on the third day. Doesn't that sound like the New Testament admonition in *I John 3:3, "And every man that hath this hope in him purifieth himself even as He is pure."* What hope is John talking about in his epistle? You have to go back to *Verse 2* which says *"Beloved, now are we the sons of God and it doth yet not appear what we shall be, but we know that when He shall APPEAR, we shall be like Him, for we shall see Him as He is."* Again let me emphasize: it is His APPEARING, not the saints disappearing!!

So the children of Israel were told, *"Be ready on the third day"* because Yahweh God was going to appear and *"every eye was going to behold him."* Where? There in the wilderness – not way off, somewhere yonder in the sky! God was going to show Himself in the earth! So what happens next? Look at *Exodus 19:16, "And it came to pass on the third day in the morning, that there were thunders and lightnings, and a thick cloud upon the mount and the voice of the TRUMPET exceedingly loud"* (notice, as in *I Thessalonians 4:16*, here in *Exodus* we find a trumpet) *"so that all the people that were in the camp trembled."* By the way, where was the cloud? Not up in heaven but on the mount!

Please read *Verse 17* slowly, *"And Moses brought forth the people out of the camp TO MEET WITH GOD."* (emphasis added). Where were they? In the air suspended in astral projection? No! *"And they stood at the lower part of the mount."* Why? Because in *Verse 11* the Word says that, *"the Lord will COME DOWN in the sight of all the people."*

It gets even better! Remember we're looking for the *"coming of the Lord"* and the words SHOUT, TRUMPET and CAUGHT UP. I will emphasize and capitalize the words in the next 3 verses. Look, and if you need to, get your own Bible and read with me *Exodus 19:18-20. Verse 18, "And Mount Sinai was altogether in a smoke because the Lord DESCENDED upon it in fire"* (as on the Day of Pentecost in *Acts 2:1-4,* when 120 believers had tongues of fire sit upon them because the Holy Spirit DESCENDED*) "and the smoke thereof ascended as the smoke of a furnace and the whole mount quaked greatly." Verse 19, "And when the voice of the TRUMPET sounded long and became louder and louder, Moses spoke and God answered him by a voice."* SHOUT! Please carefully read and reread *Verse 20.* Look what it says! The language is very similar to *I Thessalonians 4:16-18.* Here it is. *Verse 20. "And the Lord CAME DOWN* (descended) *upon the top of the mount and Moses WENT UP* (CAUGHT UP). *"* For what purpose? To meet with God! Did he leave the earth? No! Did God come down? Yes! Why? To give Moses the law, so He could have a Kingdom people, a representation nation, a holy nation on the earth, to be His *"peculiar treasure," Exodus 19:5.*

God is After a Treasure

That's why the parable in *Matthew 13:44* is given. In just one verse this parable begins to make sense. Come on; follow with me. *Verse 44, "Again the Kingdom of heaven is like treasure."* (That's you and me - God's Kingdom people) *"hidden in a field."* (What's the field? The field is the world) *Verse 38, "Which when a man hath found, he hideth and for the joy of it goeth and selleth all that he hath and buyeth that field."* What was the man after? The field? No. He was after the treasure! So to insure He would get the treasure, He purchased the whole field. Our Great and Marvelous Father paid for the whole world through Jesus' death on the cross to guarantee He would get the treasure! What does *II Corinthians 4:7* say? *"But we have this treasure in earthen vessels, that the excellency of the power may be of God and not of us."* What a marvelous grace! Our Heavenly Father placed the treasure in YOU, right in the heart of you! Jesus paid for it, and He is going to get it.

Would you like to be blessed even further? The Greek word for 'treasure' in *II Corinthians 4:7* is 'thesauros' and is translated 'wealth' or 'deposit'. Have you ever used Roget's Thesaurus? What does a thesaurus do? It expands the meaning of a word. God took His word and planted it in your earthen vessel. You are not inadequate or unequal for the task. You have a "thesaurus" inside of you. His Word is working mightily in you. Our Heavenly Father has partnered with your limitations. No wonder the scripture declares *"Eye hath not seen, ear hath not heard, neither hath entered the heart of man the things that God hath prepared for them that love Him but God hath revealed them to us by His Spirit, for the Spirit searcheth all things, yea the deep things of God." (I Corinthians 2:9, 10)* Never underestimate the treasure within you!

Chapter 7

Let's Look At The Clouds: God's Manifest Presence

Before we go on to other Biblical examples, and there are many, let us for a moment consider the phrase in *I Thessalonians 4:17, "Then we who are alive and remain shall be caught up with them "IN THE CLOUDS."* (emphasis added) Would you for a moment look at some salient verses concerning the phrase "IN THE CLOUDS?"

Practically all the verses I will quote with the word 'CLOUD' refers to God's glory. Where is it seen? Let's look.

First, *Exodus 16:10, "And it came to pass as Aaron spoke unto the whole congregation of the children of Israel, that they looked toward the wilderness and behold the GLORY of the Lord appeared in the CLOUD."* (emphasis added). Where did they see the cloud? In the earth!

Another passage in *Exodus 24:15-18, "And Moses went up into the mount and a CLOUD covered the mount." Verse 16, "And the GLORY of the Lord abode upon Mount Sinai and the CLOUD covered it six days; and the seventh day He called unto Moses out of the midst of the CLOUD." Verse 17, "And the sight of the GLORY of the Lord was like devouring fire on the top of the Mount in the eyes of the children of Israel." Verse 18, "And Moses went into the midst of the CLOUD and got up into the mount and Moses was in the mount 40 days and 40 nights."* (emphasis added). Do you get the picture? Sure, Moses was caught up in the glory cloud but he never left the earth. Please show me where we have to go up 5,000 feet, 20,000 feet or 45,000 feet to be caught up in the glory cloud.

I find in *Leviticus 16:2* a verse that tells us exactly where God met with His people! Let's find out if it's up in the atmosphere high above the earth. Read carefully *Verse 2, "And the Lord said unto Moses, "Speak unto Aaron thy brother, that he come not at all times into the holy place within the veil before the mercy seat which is upon the ark; that he die not: for I WILL APPEAR IN THE CLOUD UPON THE MERCY SEAT"* (emphasis added).

We're Going to See the King

Where was God going to appear? In the earth, in Israel's camp, in the glory cloud, in an earthly tabernacle, upon the mercy seat, the cloud of His Presence between the cherubim! Visible! They were eyewitnesses to His Majesty!!!

I ask you, "How high up do you have to go to be with Him in the clouds?" Let *Deuteronomy 31:15* answer that question, *"And the Lord appeared IN the tabernacle IN a PILLAR OF A CLOUD and the PILLAR OF THE CLOUD stood over the door of the tabernacle."* (emphasis added). If a door is usually 8 feet tall and the cloud was over the door, it wasn't very high off the ground. It was within their reach. The CLOUD appeared long ago and the CLOUD of HIS GLORY will yet appear again; sooner than we think!

> **Why do we make complex what God has already done in Biblical history?**

How I praise God that He declared so long ago He would appear not over the "judgment" seat but over the "mercy" seat. I feel it is essential at this point to reiterate how important it is for us to remain teachable. Are you able to move with the cloud of His Presence or are your tent pegs hammered too deep and rigid you couldn't move even if you wanted to? The cost would be too great. What cost? Our intellectual pride, our denominational persuasion, and our theological positions. They become more important than moving on with God.

You see, once a false teaching has been embraced, it's hard to let it go. All sacred cows must be sacrificed. None are worthy to hold on to. Believe me, I'm not picking on anyone. But because of the geographic area I live in, let me make a point and an illustration with the Baptists. First let me say, I believe most Baptists love the Lord and I'm not condescending when I say that. It's a statement of fact. They really do love the Lord and work and labor to get folks "saved," and that is to their credit.

Did you ever think that the Apostle Paul had to persuade Baptists in his day there was more than just getting saved and water baptism? Before we probe further into the "Cloud" scriptures, pause with me and read *Acts 19:1-7, "And it came to pass, that while Apollos was at Corinth, Paul having passed through the upper coasts came to Ephesus and finding certain disciples,"* Verse 2, *"He said unto them, Have you received the Holy Spirit since ye believed? And they said unto him, we have not so much as heard whether there is any Holy Spirit."* Verse 3, *"And he said unto them, Unto what then were ye baptized? And they said, Unto John's baptism."* Verse 4, *"Then said Paul, John verily baptized with the baptism of repentance saying unto the people that they should believe on Him who should come after him, that is Christ Jesus."* Verse 5, *"When they heard this, they were baptized in the Name of the Lord Jesus."* Verse 6, *"And when Paul laid his hands upon them the Holy Spirit came on them and they spoke with tongues and prophesied."* Verse 7, *"And all the men were about twelve."*

God Has More For You

What does this scripture teach us? Primarily there's more that God has for us than we presently possess. These men were Baptists! You ask, "They were?" Why, sure. They were baptized unto John's baptism. They were even called by his moniker, his nickname, John the <u>Baptist</u>. The sad fact is that John was an Old Testament prophet. Really? Why sure. John lived on the Old Testament side of the cross. John had his head cut off before Calvary, before Jesus shed His blood, before redemption was complete, before the resurrection, before the day of Pentecost, which scholars agree generally was the birthday of the church. Does that lessen John's ministry? John's impact on the nation? John's mighty ministry? The answer to these questions are No! No! No!

But when Jesus was raised from the dead, He told the disciples (*Acts 1:8*) to wait for the *"Promise of the Father"* and they would be baptized, not with John's baptism but with the Holy Spirit baptism. You see there's always more. Why label yourself to a past move of God? Why limit yourself to any denomination? Move with the CLOUD of His guidance and authority.

In the process of your spiritual development, God will take you through transition periods to remove old ways, old ideas and old traditions to bring you into the new.

I would ask you at this time to pause for a moment before we go further into the "CLOUD" scriptures and simply touch your eyes and pray, "Lord, open my eyes to new things, new insights." Touch your ears and request of the Father, "Lord, let me hear what the Spirit's saying to the church." Lay your hand upon your heart and say, "Father, unveil truth to my hearing heart." He will honor the seeking heart...the hungry spirit...the yearning truth-seeker. I declare to you, He will.

Moving to a Greater Glory

Let's go on in our pursuit of understanding more about what it means to be *"caught up together with them in the <u>CLOUDS</u>."* To tell you the truth, I've searched other men's writings and have not found much they have had to say about this subject. There's just not much written about it. Do you think Peter, James and John were privileged when they saw the glory on the Mount of Transfiguration? I think most of you would agree they were certainly privileged! Even Peter calls it excellent glory and went on to preface it by declaring that they were *"eyewitnesses of His majesty."* *II Peter 1:16-18, "For we have not followed cunningly devised fables, when we made known unto you the power and coming of our Lord Jesus Christ,*

47

but were eyewitnesses of his majesty." Verse 17, "For he received from God the Father honor and glory, when there came such a voice to him from the excellent glory, This is my beloved Son, in whom I am well pleased." Verse 18, "And this voice which came from heaven we heard, when we were with him in the holy mount."

Let's look at Luke's account of this tremendous experience in *Luke 9:29-35,* *"And as he prayed, the fashion of his countenance was altered, and his raiment was white and glistering." Verse 30, "And, behold, there talked with him two men, which were Moses and Elijah." Verse 31, "Who appeared in glory, and spake of his decease which he should accomplish at Jerusalem." Verse 32, "But Peter and they that were with him were heavy with sleep: and when they were awake, they saw his glory, and the two men that stood with him." Verse 33, "And it came to pass, as they departed from him, Peter said unto Jesus, Master, it is good for us to be here: and let us make three tabernacles; one for thee, and one for Moses, and one for Elijah, not knowing what he said." Verse 34, "While he thus spake, <u>there came a cloud, and overshadowed them: and they feared as they entered into the cloud</u>." Verse 35, "And there came a voice out of the cloud, saying, This is my beloved Son: hear him."*

Please look at *Verse 34* again. What does it say about the cloud? It says, *"it overshadowed them."* That sure sounds like *Psalms 91:1, "He that dwelleth in the secret place of the Most High shall abide under the <u>shadow</u> of the Almighty."* Could it be the three disciples were in the "secret place?" The next phrase of *Verse 34* leaps out at you and declares, *"and they feared as they entered into the <u>CLOUD</u>."* Where were they? On the mountain!

Did they leave the earth? No! Did they witness the glory of God? Yes! Were they caught up together with <u>them</u> in the cloud? Yes! Who is the <u>them</u>? Why, it was Elijah and Moses and Jesus! Did it require that they go some place way up in the sky? No, of course not. God revealed His glory to three men and they didn't have to leave the earth to do it. Why do we make complex what God has already done in Biblical history?

Old Testament Saints Entered Into the Glory Cloud

Would you examine with me three scriptures from the book of *Numbers.* As you read and study, pay careful attention to the location of the cloud. Ask yourself, "Can I be caught up in the CLOUD of His Glory – in the CLOUD of His divine guidance? Can it happen in the day in which we live?"

Numbers 10:34-36, "And the cloud of the Lord <u>was upon them</u> by day, when they went out of the camp." Verse 35, "And it came to pass, *when the ark set forward, that Moses said, Rise up, Lord, and let thine enemies be scattered; and let them that hate thee flee before thee." Verse 36, "And when it rested, he said, Return, O Lord, unto the many thousands of Israel."*

Isn't it interesting? *Verse 34* says the cloud was upon them by day. *Verse 35* talks about the Ark of God's Presence scattering God's enemies. Let me ask you "where is the ark today?" Right inside of you! Why don't you lift up your voice like a TRUMPET right now and SHOUT the praises of our God and be CAUGHT UP to the throne of His glorious Presence? Take a few moments and enter into the glory cloud.

Look further now at *Numbers 11:24-25, "And Moses went out, and told the people the words of the Lord, and gathered the seventy men of the elders of the people, and set them round about the tabernacle." Verse 25, "And the Lord came down in a cloud, and spake unto him, and took of the spirit that was upon him, and gave it unto the seventy elders: and it came to pass, that, when the spirit rested upon them, they prophesied, and did not cease."* Do you see the picture described here in 2 verses? 70 elders round about the tabernacle. *Verse 25* says *"the Lord came down in a <u>CLOUD</u>."* Did they ever leave the earth? No! Isn't it wonderful to think that our God comes down to where we are? What takes place when He comes down? He manifests His Spirit and His Glory! Begin to be aware of His glory coming down. The end of the verse is awesome and spectacular. It says, *"the Spirit rested upon them, they prophesied, and did not cease."* Hallelujah! The purpose of the "cloud" is God's Spirit resting upon us, using us to prophecy and blessing us ceaselessly.

Look at one more verse in *Numbers 14:14, "And they will tell it to the inhabitants of this land for they have heard that Thou Lord <u>art among</u> this people, that Thou Lord <u>art seen</u> face to face and that Thy <u>CLOUD</u> standeth <u>OVER</u> them, and that Thou goest before them by daytime in a pillar of a CLOUD and in a pillar of fire by night."*

Are you open to new ideas? Can you see in the above verses the possibility exists to have a different point of view about being "caught up in the CLOUDS?" When a person admits their former interpretation is something passed on and not thought through, that person is becoming teachable. Why not question institutional standards? Why not open the door of your mind to more than just traditional interpretation? Are you going to embrace the ways of men that remain stale and old, or will you admit to God and yourself that you hunger for truth and righteousness?

Are you willing to be shackled with obsolete songs like, "I'll see you in the Rapture" or be content in putting a bumper sticker on your vehicle declaring it will be unmanned when the "rapture" occurs? The greatest enemy to truth and reality is religious professionalism. Millions of good people are deceived. Millions clutch their religious trinkets and toys and TVs as if these things were going to save them.

What is the purpose for writing about CLOUDS...SHOUT...TRUMPET... CAUGHT UP? Why even try to counter popular beliefs that would have evoked ridicule and laughter a century ago? The answer is simple. This little book is written for the <u>remnant</u>; it is written to prepare you for battle! My plea and urgent request to you is not for you to look up pleadingly to the eastern sky for it to split so you can leave, but to watch, pray, occupy, fulfill the great commission and make disciples. If you're looking for something, at least look for a CLOUD of protection, provision and power.

Let us obey the command of *Deuteronomy 31:6-8,15*, which declares, *"Be strong and of good courage, fear not nor be afraid of them: for the Lord thy God, He it is who doth go with thee; He will not fail thee nor forsake thee." Verse 7, "And Moses called unto Joshua and said unto him in the sight of all Israel, Be strong and of good courage, for thou must go with this people unto the land which the Lord hath sworn unto their fathers to give them, and thou shalt cause them to inherit it." Verse 8, "And the Lord, He it is who doth go before thee, He will be with thee, He will not fail thee neither forsake thee, fear not, neither be dismayed."* What powerful words! What tremendous encouragement! Now look at *Verse 15*. God is about to make an appearance. Where will He appear and when He does, what will He do? Take all of the children of Israel to heaven to live? No! He had just told them in the previous verses that Joshua was going to cause the people to inherit the earth. I pray to God we would have leadership like that today! Look where the Almighty appears. *Verse 15, "And the Lord appeared in the tabernacle in a pillar of a <u>CLOUD</u>; and the pillar of the CLOUD <u>stood over the door</u> of the tabernacle."*(emphasis added).

I ask again "where was the cloud?" Not far away from them but in the very center of their camp about 8 to 10 feet off the ground. Beloved, the <u>cloud</u> of His glory is in our midst and that CLOUD is a witness you are going to inherit the earth, not fly away to heaven. No escape routes! No shortcuts! No "stop the earth, I want to get off!"

Nehemiah states even the rebellion and hard-heartedness of God's people could not keep the CLOUD of God's Presence out of their midst. Remember these people were not heathen; they were God's example nation, His holy people. Do you know what this shows me? There's hope for us! Read the following verses from *Nehemiah 9:12-20*, but especially *Verse 19*. *Verse 12, "Moreover thou leddest them in the day by a cloudy pillar; and in the night by a pillar of fire, to give them light in the way wherein they should go." Verse 13, "Thou camest down also upon mount Sinai, and spakest with them from heaven, and gavest them right judgments, and true laws, good statutes and commandments." Verse 14, "And madest known unto them thy holy sabbath, and commandedst them precepts, statutes, and laws, by the hand of Moses thy servant:" Verse 15, "And gavest them bread from heaven for their hunger, and broughtest forth water for them out of the rock for their thirst, and promisedst them that they should go in to possess the land which thou hadst sworn to give them." Verse 16, "But they and our fathers dealt proudly, and hardened their necks, and hearkened not to thy commandments." Verse 17, "And refused to obey, neither were mindful of thy wonders that thou didst among them; but hardened their necks, and in their rebellion appointed a captain to return to their bondage: but thou art a God ready to pardon, gracious and merciful, slow to anger, and of great kindness, and forsookest them not." Verse 18, "Yea, when they had made them a molten calf, and said, This is thy god that brought thee up out of Egypt, and had wrought great provocations;" Verse 19, "Yet thou in thy manifold mercies forsookest them not in the wilderness: the pillar of the cloud departed not from them by day, to lead them in the way; neither the pillar of fire by night, to show them light, and the way wherein they should go." Verse 20, "Thou gavest also thy good spirit to instruct them, and withheldest not thy manna from their mouth, and gavest them water for their thirst."*

Even though they erected false gods, even though they refused to obey, even though they wanted to return to beggardly elements of bondage, did our kind and loving Heavenly Father remove the CLOUD? No! What long-suffering and what mercy! Even in our waywardness, He is faithful!

There are many other scriptures that deal with the subject of "cloud(s)." Since I have desired to awaken an interest in the subject, here are a few references you can look up and study on your own: *I Kings 8:10-11; Psalms 105:37-39; Isaiah 4:5; Exodus 40:34-38; I Corinthians 10:1-2 and Revelations 1:6-7.*

Chapter 8

Joshua The Soldier – Caught Up In Victory

Let's get back to the subject of SHOUT, TRUMPET and CAUGHT UP. One of the most significant and sobering stories in the entire Bible with regard to this subject is the Biblical account of the conquest of Jericho with Joshua (Yahshua) the soldier and military man, leading the people to battle. "What battle?" you ask. They simply walked around the city seven (7) days. A very important truth to reckon in your mind as you lay the facts out before you is: the <u>old</u> leadership is over - Moses is dead! It's really hard to let go of Moses. We all exclaim, "My God, look what he did!" He was raised in Pharaoh's courts, refused to be called the son of Pharaoh's daughter, chose affliction over pleasure *(Hebrews 11:24-29)*, seemingly lost to history as a shepherd in Midian's desert, relegated to taking care of his father-in-law's sheep. Ah! But one day he saw a flame in the backside of a desert, and he never rested until he saw the God of that flame! Champion of champions, he received the Ten Commandments!

> **A lot of folks see truth, but can you walk in it?**

He received manna, water from a rock and on and on we could recount stories of victory. He delivered a whole nation, but now he's gone, it's all over and the nation is in mourning. You've got to take a <u>new</u> mind, <u>new</u> direction, <u>new</u> leadership, and <u>new</u> tactics. Are you going to be able to make the painful transition from Moses to Joshua? The sad fact stares you in the face: the whole generation was <u>not</u> able to make the change. Look around. Bones are bleaching in the wilderness sand. These were good people, saved people (saved by the blood of the Passover lamb), baptized people (baptized in the water of the Red Sea), baptized in the Spirit (the cloud), but not able to move with the cloud.

I Corinthians 10:1-2, "Moreover, brethren, I would not that ye should be ignorant, how that all our fathers were under the cloud, and all passed through the sea;" Verse 2, "And were all baptized unto Moses in the cloud and in the sea."

Faith That Pleases God

All but two of that generation died. Think of it – all but Caleb and Joshua. The Bible says, *"they had another spirit"* because they followed the Lord *"fully" (Numbers 14:24)*. Is that your desire? Read on – we'll see. *Joshua 1:1-3, "Now after the death of Moses the servant of the Lord it came to pass, that the Lord spake unto Joshua the son of Nun, Moses' minister,* saying," *Verse 2, "Moses, my servant, is dead; now therefore arise, go over this Jordan, thou, and all this people, unto the land which I do give to them, even to the children of Israel." Verse 3, "Every place that the sole of your foot shall tread upon, that have I given unto you, as I said unto Moses."*

Isn't *Verse 3* interesting? It <u>doesn't</u> say, "whatever you see I'll give you." It says, *"whatever you walk in I'll give you."* It's not enough to see truth. A lot of folks see truth, but can you walk in it? Then and only then is it really yours! No wonder that first chapter of *Joshua* says four (4) times in *Verses 6-7, 9* and *18* to *"be strong and of good courage."*

Success That Pleases God

One other wonderful and powerful truth is this: only one time in the whole Bible is the word "success" mentioned and it's here in *Joshua 1:8, "This book of the law shall not depart out of thy mouth; but thou shalt meditate therein day and night that thou mayest observe to <u>DO</u> according to all that is written therein: for then thou shalt make thy way prosperous, and then thou shalt have good <u>SUCCESS</u>."* (emphasis added). With all the 'success' seminars, the 'prosperity' emphasis permeating our society, culture and churches, isn't it particularly engaging when you think that God's holy Word only mentions 'success' once? And the one and only time it does appear, it has to do with obedience to His holy law? Do you wish to be successful? What God considers "successful" and what society considers "successful" are worlds apart. *Luke 16:15, "And he said unto them, Ye are they which justify yourselves before men; but God knoweth your hearts: for that which is highly esteemed among men is abomination in the sight of God."*

With Yahweh's definition of "success" in our thinking, let's go on to the conquest of Jericho with the thought of "observe to do" or to put it in the words of that old hymn:

> **"Trust and obey**
>
> **for there's no other way,**
>
> **to be happy in Jesus,**
>
> **but to trust and obey."**

Let's go to *Chapter 6* and find those most pronounced words that *I Thessalonians 4:16-17* states, we are emphasizing, namely "SHOUT, TRUMPET and CAUGHT UP." Remember also, we're not talking about <u>leaving</u> but <u>staying</u>, hence the title of the book is "I want to be Left Behind." Let's read on.

Joshua 6:1-5, "Now Jericho was securely shut up because of the children of Israel: none went out and none came in." Verse 2, "And the Lord said unto Joshua, "See, I have given into thy hand Jericho and its king and the mighty men of valor." Verse 3, "And ye shall compass the city all ye men of war and go round about the city once. Thus shall ye do six days." Verse 4, "And seven priests shall bear before the ark seven TRUMPETS of rams' horns: and the seventh day ye shall compass the city seven times, and the priests shall blow with the TRUMPETS." Verse 5, "And it shall come to pass, that when they make a long blast with the ram's horn, and when ye hear the sound of the TRUMPET, all the people shall SHOUT with a great SHOUT; and the wall of the city shall fall down flat, and the people shall ASCEND UP (CAUGHT UP) every man straight before him." (emphasis added).

I would strongly urge you to read the whole chapter several times before proceeding. This is the awesome conquest of Canaan. This was land... their inheritance, not heaven. Does this mean I don't believe in heaven? Of course not, but heaven is not the subject right now. This was what God promised Abraham's holy seed through faith.

Romans 4:13, "For the promise that he should be heir of the WORLD (emphasis added) *was not to Abraham or to his seed through the law but through the righteousness of faith."*

Do you long to see God's Kingdom on earth? How did it happen in *Joshua 6*? Well, first look at the promise of *Verse 2*. God gave the city, the king, the mighty men of valor into the hand of Joshua and the children of Israel. We're talking about land, positions of authority, political spheres. Let me ask you a question. Think it over carefully. Let's just propose and offer a consideration for you to ponder. What would you do differently from what's being done today if the Kingdom were put in place tomorrow, given to you to run and the Lord put you in as an administrator of His Kingdom? Didn't He say if you were faithful to Him that depending on your gifts and talents, you would rule over 10 cities or 5 cities? (See *Luke 19:17,19*.) I think it's time we re-evaluate our thinking or our traditions.

Go with me now to *Joshua 6:20* and I will comment or ask questions after each brief quotation of scripture. Here we go. *Verse 20, "So the people SHOUTED."* (emphasis added). Where were they? In heaven? No! They were on the earth. When did they SHOUT? *"When the priests blew with the TRUMPETS."* (emphasis added). A "trumpet" in the Bible is symbolic of a message. You ask, "really?" Sure! What does *I Corinthians 14:8* say? *"For if the trumpet give an uncertain sound, who shall prepare himself to the battle?"* To the what? To the BATTLE! That's spelled B-A-T-T-L-E!!

You see the message of this book is <u>battle</u>. I'm blowing on the TRUMPET "REVEILLE, WAKE UP." Wake up to truth! Wake up to your calling! Wake up to <u>do</u> battle! I'm certainly not blowing "taps" or the sound of "<u>retreat</u>." To tell you the truth, most folks today in this casper milque toast mentality would prefer the sleepy time lullaby of "nothing bad is going to happen to me because I'm God's special pet." Are you a sissy or a soldier? If you are a soldier, then act like one. As the Apostle Paul said, *"Endure hardness as a good soldier." (II Timothy 2:3)*

Let's get back to *Verse 20, "and it came to pass <u>when</u> the people heard the sound of the trumpet and the people SHOUTED with a great SHOUT that the wall fell down flat."* (emphasis added). The key words are SHOUT, TRUMPET and CAUGHT UP. Are you finding them here? Yes! Victory is assured. Follow the battle plan! Get involved in the march of obedience! SHOUT with the voice of triumph! For six days *("a day with the Lord is as a thousand years" - II Peter 3:8)* Godly people have marched on this <u>earth</u> and more is going to be accomplished in the seventh day than in the previous six days because on the seventh day, God's people march around the city seven (7) times. More ground is covered, more insight and more revelation is given. My, what a reason to "SHOUT!" No wonder *Revelation 18:2* declares, *"And he cried mightily with a strong voice* (does that sound like "SHOUT?") *saying Babylon* (Jericho) *the great is fallen, is fallen."* And how about *Revelation 18:20* which goes on to say, *"Rejoice over her, thou heaven and ye holy apostles and prophets; for God hath avenged you on her."* Verse 21, *"And a mighty angel took up a stone like a great millstone, and cast it into the sea saying "Thus with violence shall that great city Babylon* (Jericho) *be thrown down and shall be found no more at all."* The entire next chapter, *(Revelation 19)* has to do with the battle of praise and worship.

Please go back with me to *Joshua 6:20* to the phrase *"that the wall fell down flat."* My goodness, look what happens next. After the SHOUT brings the walls of Jericho (Babylon) down, what takes place? The scripture goes on to say, *"The people <u>went up</u>."* Do you get it? They were CAUGHT UP!! Not to heaven, for your Bible says, *"They went into the city every man straight before him and they took the city."* What did they take? A mansion over the hilltop? No! A thousand times No! They took Jericho, its king and its mighty men of valor. They possessed what God promised them! The earth is being restored to its rightful custodians – God's children. Do you see that this Old Testament passage about the fall of Jericho's walls has in it the language of *I Thessalonians 4:16-17* and that just perhaps the present "church complacent" will become the "church militant?" Any careful Bible student will realize God is glorified when we fight the *"good fight of faith,"* not when we "cut and run." Put your faith and trust in God who tells us in *Ephesians 6:13, "that ye may be able to <u>withstand</u> in the evil day, and having done all to <u>stand</u>."* Did you get that? After having done ALL, did He say, get raptured out? No! He said, "STAND." That means you're going to be here! That's exactly the reason why...

"I WANT TO BE LEFT BEHIND!"

"Are you looking for a majority of the people to endorse this viewpoint," you ask me. Well, let me ask you a question before I answer you. Can you show me any time in Biblical history where God used a majority to bring victory and deliverance from bondage? Well, you can't! It's just not there. But the Bible has much to say about a Godly remnant. So I'm not looking for that indifferent, apathetic, rebellious majority. But in the face of myriad obstacles, let a holy remnant build an altar and place themselves upon it. That's where I desire to be. What about you? Are you stuck in the tradition or teaching of a past move of God? By the way, that is a good definition of a denomination (a monument to a past move of God).

Chapter 9

Sing A Song Of Deliverance – Caught Up In Music

Before we look at one of my Biblical heroes whom I like to refer to as, "God's Invincible Weakling," let's sing a song. You put the music to it. I'll give you the words. This song was written a while ago, quite a while ago, like maybe 2,700 years ago. You put the melody to it. Guess what? It's got the language of *I Thessalonians 4:16-17* in it. That's right. "SHOUT, TRUMPET, CAUGHT UP." Let's sing!

> *Psalms 47:1-9, "O clap your hands, all ye people; shout unto God with the voice of triumph." Verse 2, "For the Lord most high is terrible; He is a great King over all the earth." Verse 3, "He shall subdue the people under us, and the nations under our feet." Verse 4, "He shall choose our inheritance for us, the excellency of Jacob whom he loved. Selah." Verse 5, "God is GONE UP with a SHOUT, the Lord with the sound of a TRUMPET." (emphasis added). Verse 6, "Sing praises to God, sing praises: sing praises unto our King, sing praises." Verse 7, "For God is the King of all the earth: sing ye praises with understanding." Verse 8, "God reigneth over the heathen: God sitteth upon the throne of his holiness." Verse 9, "The princes of the people are gathered together, even the people of the God of Abraham: for the shields of the earth belong unto God: he is greatly exalted."*

Did you do what I asked you to do? What do I mean? Did you read it? Probably 99% of you read it. Let's go back to *Verse 6*. What does it say? *"Sing praises to God, sing praises; sing praises unto our King, sing praises."* Do you get it? Four times in one verse you're told to sing. What do you think God is trying to get you to do? Now go back and sing the Psalm. Sing it from your heart! Make melody in your spirit. While you're singing, do what the song says. Clap, shout, sing and exalt Him! I'll wager you couldn't get through verse one without laughing or at least smiling. You see, worship, praise and singing makes the heart glad.

This *47th Psalm* is a song of warfare praise. Look at *Verse 1*. After the admonition to *"clap your hands"* and give applause to the One who is worthy, our great and awe-inspiring King, the next word is "SHOUT." *Verse 2* declares that His dominion, power, authority, Kingship and jurisdiction is *"over all the EARTH."* The next verse intimates that we are "CAUGHT UP" for please notice where the people are; under us, and the nations are under our feet. Without stretching or straining to make this certain thought fit, if they are under you, where does that place you?

"CAUGHT UP!" And if you feel this is improper exegesis then look at Verse 5, *"God is <u>gone up</u> (CAUGHT UP) with a SHOUT, the Lord with the sound of a TRUMPET."*(emphasis added).

Here in the *Psalms*, the songbook of God's people, the theme "SHOUT, TRUMPET, CAUGHT UP" can be the vehicle that will propel you out of limited and restricted understanding. *Verse 7* declares, *"For God is the King of all the EARTH; sing ye praises with understanding."* How many times have we made the declaration "Jesus is the King of Kings and He is the Lord of Lords?" What Kings is He King of? Are we talking about earthly monarchs? Of course not. There are a limited number of earthly monarchs today. How many would you say? There probably are no more than 25 or 30. Well, could it be that *Revelation 5:10* gives us an answer. Quote it out loud with me, *"And hast made us unto our God, kings and priests and <u>WE SHALL REIGN ON THE EARTH.</u>"* (emphasis added). Quote it again! Can it be true? It's better than what we ever dreamed of or imagined! My friend, He is the King of other kings and wonder of wonders, you're selected for kingship. He's talking about you. You're one of those kings He's King of.

Again, I declare to you while others have "leaving on their mind" and flying off to that "supper in the sky," <u>I WANT TO BE LEFT BEHIND</u>. Why? Read the last part of *Revelation 5:10, "and WE SHALL REIGN ON THE EARTH."*(emphasis added).

Chapter 10

Gideon – God's Invincible Weakling – Caught Up In Battle

Gideon - God's Invincible Weakling

Judges Chapters 6 and 7

One of the allied purposes of this treatise is to deliver God's people from not only a narrow, prejudiced perspective of popular faulty futurism but to get you, the student of scripture, loosed from a spirit of fear. Intimidation can be terrorizing for *"fear has torment."* *(I John 4:18)* Before God could use Gideon as a worship-warrior, He had to eliminate the fear factor.

There is a process and progression that our wise and Holy God institutes to fulfill His noble designs and purposes in the vessels of His choosing. There are no raw recruits or vacillating volunteers in this portion of Holy Writ. Go ahead; look through the entire history of God's choosing and equipping deliverers. How many volunteers do you find? How long is the line? Does the queue circle the block? No, dear reader, the truth is: God chooses and conscripts men and women against their will. He may not allow you to be invited to the big anointing service like David of old. As a matter of fact, the very point that David wasn't included to come to the "big meeting" is the very sign and indication that God had singled him out for sovereign dealings yet to be revealed. Ah, yes, Samuel, doesn't Eliab look good, all dressed up in his military uniform, ready to be anointed? But the whisper of the Spirit of God to Samuel's heart that day, as he was unscrewing the cap on the horn of oil, was *"don't look on the outward appearance" (I Samuel 16:7).*

> **God takes great joy in working through the "remnant."**

Measure Up to God's Standard

You see when man measures man he puts the tape around the man's head, but when God measures man He puts the tape around man's heart. David's heart was filled with praise, adoration and worship while taking care of a few sheep (see *I Samuel 17:28*). Were David's older brothers excited about the anointing on their younger brother? No! The opposite was true. They were callous, critical, sneering and snobbish (see *I Samuel 17:29-30*). But, all the while, the anointing was working and more importantly, God was watching. God anoints worshippers and that's the bottom line.

In our search for volunteers for difficult tasks and demanding times, ask about Moses in Midian's desert taking care of a few sheep. Did he volunteer? No! Not at all. You may as well laugh when asking about Joseph. Who would stand in line to be sold into slavery? Harsh, hellish, cruel treatment. Not me. Maligned? Misunderstood? Count me out! A long, long, prison term? No way! I'm afraid not! However, God's ways and His choice will stand! So now we ask the questions: why choose Gideon and what are the steps to eliminate fear in his life?

Fear Not, Little Flock

From God's initial contact with Gideon as he was threshing wheat at the winepress to hide it from the Midianites to the very night of the battle, (now, listen to me) I'm telling you, to the very night of the battle, there was fear in Gideon's life. Let me ask you a question: how do we, God's people, get rid of fear? The answer will surprise you! First let's list the scriptures where fear is mentioned or at least intimated in Gideon's life.

Judges 6:10, "FEAR NOT (emphasis added) *the gods of the Amorites in whose land ye dwell."* This is an admonition to get rid of fear.

Judges 6:11, "Gideon threshed wheat by the winepress TO HIDE IT (emphasis added) *from the Midianites."* "OK," you say, "I can see by the text that he was fearful."

Judges 6:22-23, "And when Gideon perceived that he was an angel of the Lord, Gideon said, Alas, O Lord God! for because I have seen an angel of the Lord face to face." Verse 23, "And the Lord said unto him, Peace be unto thee; FEAR NOT: thou shalt not die." (emphasis added). Why would the Lord admonish Gideon not to fear if it wasn't present in his life? You can probably see validity as you deduce this scripture reference.

Judges 6:27, "Then Gideon took ten men of his servants, and did as the Lord had said unto him: and so it was, because HE FEARED (emphasis added) *his father's household, and the men of the city, that he could not do it by day, that he did it by night."* Gideon was fearful of peer pressure and family harassment.

Judges 7:3, "Now therefore go to, proclaim in the ears of the people, saying, Whosoever IS FEARFUL AND AFRAID, (emphasis added) *let him return and depart early from mount Gilead. And there returned of the people twenty and two thousand; and there remained ten thousand."*

Gideon probably wanted to leave because he lost 2/3 of his army. But Yahweh Almighty knew that Gideon had to eliminate the fearful soldiers for they would contaminate the entire army. Gideon's duty was to get rid of the fearful no matter what the outcome. So what if everyone leaves? Our duty is crystal clear no matter what the outcome. God is more interested in the character of faith standing alone than in amassing a humanistic scheme of a democratic majority. Can you stand alone while the majority desert you? Can you?

Judges 7:6-8, "And the number of them that lapped, putting their hand to their mouth, were three hundred men: but all the rest of the people bowed down upon their knees to drink water." Verse 7, "And the Lord said unto Gideon, By the three hundred men that lapped will I save you, and deliver the Midianites into thine hand: and let all the other people go every man unto his place." Verse 8, "So the people took victuals in their hand, and their trumpets: and he sent all the rest of Israel every man unto his tent, and retained those three hundred men: and the host of Midian was beneath him in the valley." By the time the water test is complete, Gideon has less than 1% of the original number of 32,000. He is left with 300 men; 31,700 were disqualified – 22,000 were fearful and 9,700 failed the water test. You ask, "what water test?" Why, getting down on all fours and lapping water any old way you want. Get this and mark it well in your spirit! Only 300, again, I repeat only 300, got on bended knee and brought the water up to their mouth by cupping their hand. Dipping their hand in the water, they brought the water of the word (*Ephesians 5:26*) by the "hand ministry" to their mouth (i.e. the 5-fold ministry of the apostle, prophet, evangelist, pastor and teacher) (*Ephesians 4:11-12*) to be refreshed with revelation God-knowledge. That's what qualifies you – approaching the waters of truth the proper way. No wonder Gideon's knees had what I call Belshazzeritis (knees smiting one another). He lost over 99% of his congregation. Think of it: 300 out of 32,000. Talk about starting with a "mega-church" and left with a paltry 300. But God takes great joy in working through the "remnant." That way He gets all the glory!

"Before we see that Gideon had fear even the <u>very</u> night of the battle, notice with me, this: God always begins his dealings with His people by sending His trouble-shooters, the prophets. Look around the traditional churches today. The prophet's chair is empty. The reason is clear - most churches today are 501 C-3 non-prophet organizations."

Go back with me to *Judges 6:1, "And the children of Israel did evil in the sight of the Lord."* I ask you, "Has anything changed?" What was the result? Bondage (*Verse 2*), enemy infiltration (*Verse 3*), gross national products robbed and destroyed (*Verse 4*), illegal immigration (*Verse 5*), poverty (*Verse 6*). What is the result of this affliction? A turning back to God (*Verse 7*).

The Beginning of Deliverance

So what does God do? He initiates His first line of defense. He sends them a prophet. Does this sound like a principle of scripture? Read *Amos 3:6-7*, *"Shall a TRUMPET be blown in the city and the people not be afraid? Shall there be calamity in a city and the Lord hath not done it?" Verse 7, "Surely the Lord God will do nothing, but He revealeth His secret unto His servants, the PROPHETS."* (emphasis added).

Today we've got a lot of religious hypocrisy. Oh yes, we've got presidents, superintendents and archbishops. We're up to date with man-made dogmas and doctrines. Doesn't it even bother you a little that the word "RAPTURE" isn't even found in your Bible? We offer, "Well, this is the way I was raised" or "this is what our denomination believes" or "this is what Dr. J. Flavius Fluffyhead teaches." We seem to think that what Jesus has said about it doesn't matter. Our attitude is "don't disturb me, I'm enjoying my ostrich-like head stuck in the sands of men's traditions." This is a warning to all prophets: "Pledge your head to heaven because men will take it off." Also, there are invisible signs over the doors of most traditional churches: "Do NOT disturb, business as usual." Meanwhile, the impact of lukewarm, cautious, polite and professional religious societies are negligible. Christian television offers the promise of material gain. Do not talk about subjects that make people uncomfortable. Why, if someone would disagree with the present day "RAPTURE" teaching, our ratings would fall. They don't tell you this but I know for a fact, so would their dollars. Please don't kid yourself. The present electronic church is competing for audience share and viewer dollars. The crying need of the hour is a fire-forged prophet like Elijah or John the Baptist, who will prepare the way of the Lord. The survival of truth depends on it! Where are the prophets with a major message? Let them step forward and confront the mind-numbing, seductive, self-interest escapism of our day. It happened in Gideon's day. Pray it will happen in our day.

Step number 2 in the development of Gideon's faith is the appearance of the angel of the Lord. Notice, after the prophet, the Angel makes His appearance. *Verse 12, "And the angel of the Lord appeared unto him and said unto him, The Lord is with thee, thou mighty man of valor."* Would to God that we would believe God's assessment and opinion of us rather than our limp and lame evaluation of what and who we are. The angel said Gideon was a *"mighty man of valor."* But what did Gideon believe about himself? Look at *Verse 15, "And he said unto Him Oh my Lord, wherewith shall I save Israel? Behold my family is poor in Manasseh and I am the least in my father's house."* Hallelujah! God delivered the nation through a poor man – and the least! Be encouraged. God doesn't need a rich man or an egomaniac. He just needs someone called, committed and confirmed.

Step number 3 is the confirmation. Gideon asks for a sign. Hold on for a moment. If I were to ask you, "What was the sign that God gave Gideon," the majority of you would reply "the fleece." And you would be wrong. For the covenant sign that God gave Gideon was Blood, Water and Spirit. That is the covenant sign of the New Testament, of Calvary. Read *I John 5:8, "And there are three that bear witness in earth, the Spirit and the water and the blood; and these three agree in one."*

Let's look at what I call the covenant sign of blood, water and Spirit. Read with me *Judges 6:17-22, "And he said unto him, If now I have found grace in thy sight, then show me a sign that thou talkest with me." Verse 18, "Depart not hence, I pray thee, until I come unto thee, and bring forth my present, and set it before thee. And he said, I will tarry until thou come again." Verse 19, "And Gideon went in, and made ready a kid, and unleavened cakes of an ephah of flour: the flesh he put in a basket, and he put the broth in a pot, and brought it out unto him under the oak, and presented it." Verse 20, "And the angel of God said unto him, Take the flesh and the unleavened cakes, and lay them upon this rock, and pour out the broth. And he did so." Verse 21, "Then the angel of the Lord put forth the end of the staff that was in his hand, and touched the flesh and the unleavened cakes; and there rose up fire out of the rock, and consumed the flesh and the unleavened cakes. Then the angel of the Lord departed out of his sight." Verse 22, "And when Gideon perceived that he was an angel of the Lord, Gideon said, Alas, O Lord God! for because I have seen an angel of the Lord face to face."*

Gideon asked for a sign in *Verse 17*. The fleece he put a request for twice doesn't occur until *Verses 36-40*. The fleece request he asked for was a definite indication of the weakness of Gideon's faith, for in *Verse 19* through *Verse 21* the true sign was given. You say to me, "Just what do you mean?" Well, go back and look at *Verse 19*. It declares that, *"Gideon went in, and made ready a kid."* What did he do? He killed it. What was shed? Blood! It also says *"he put the broth in a pot."* What's the broth symbolic of? Water. Refer now to V*erse 20*. What did the angel of the Lord tell Gideon to do? *"Take the flesh* (symbolizing the blood), *the unleavened cakes* (symbolizing truth), *lay them upon the rock* (the altar) *and pour out the broth* (the water)." The angel of the Lord then touched the flesh and cakes and what happened? FIRE came up out of the rock and consumed the flesh and the cakes. What does the fire typify? The Spirit! There you have it! Blood – Water – Spirit. Glory to God! That was the only sign Gideon needed to prepare himself for battle. This is the "absolute" sign he needed.

This is Gideon's reference point. This is power, for this sign brings Gideon (*Verse 24*) to a place of worship. That is really "ground zero." The altar of worship has always been the place where battles are won, for this is where Gideon gets conquered. He was indelibly marked by God through the covenant sign of BLOOD, WATER and SPIRIT!

You ask, "In this story of Gideon are we going to get to the correlation of *I Thessalonians 4:16,17* – you know, SHOUT, TRUMPET and CAUGHT UP?" We will, but first let me point out the incredible grace and mercy God demonstrates in this "invincible weakling." Remember, I said earlier that even though it was the very night of the battle, Gideon was fearful. My question has been, "Heavenly Father, if you sent a prophet and Gideon was still fearful, how could that be?" Then Lord, you sent an angel and he was still fearful. You gave Gideon the covenant sign. What's the answer? The answer is this; he didn't believe the prophet, the man of God. He didn't believe the Angel of the Lord. He didn't believe the covenant sign. God then says, "I must send Gideon to the enemy's camp. He will hear what the enemy says and Gideon will believe the enemy. You ask, "Is that in the Bible?" It sure is. Read with me *Judges 7:9-11, "And it came to pass the same night, that the Lord said unto him, Arise, get thee down unto the host; for I have delivered it into thine hand." Verse 10, "But if thou fear to go down, go thou with Phurah thy servant down to the host:" Verse 11, "And thou shalt hear what they say; and afterward shall thine hands be strengthened to go down unto the host. Then went he down with Phurah his servant unto the outside of the armed men that were in the host."*

Didn't *Verse 9* say *"the same night?"* That was the very night of the battle. *Verse 10* says, *"If you FEAR to go down, take Phurah thy servant."* *Verse 11* says, *"Then went he down with Phurah his servant."* It doesn't take a rocket scientist to determine by deductive reasoning that he was fearful. He took Phurah his servant! If you fear to go down, take Phurah. Amazing, isn't it? Our "invincible weakling" has clay feet. God will use weak vessels. God will use what is available.

Can you see them furtively moving about the camp of the enemy dressed in their camouflage uniforms? Moving in the shadows, finally inching up to an enemy tent, their hearts racing and pulse pounding, and then listening to the conversation inside. Here's the conversation (*Judges 7:12-14*) *"And the Midianites and the Amalekites and all the children of the east lay along in the valley like grasshoppers for multitude; and their camels were without number, as the sand by the sea side for multitude." Verse 13, "And when Gideon was come, behold, there was a man that told a dream unto his fellow, and said, Behold, I dreamed a dream, and, lo, a cake of barley bread tumbled into the host of Midian, and came unto a tent, and smote it that it fell, and overturned it, that the tent lay along."* Verse 14, *"And his fellow answered and said, This is nothing else save the sword of Gideon the son of Joash, a man of Israel: for into his hand hath God delivered Midian, and all the host."* Can you believe the dream? The enemy said they were defeated by a loaf of bread!

Didn't Jesus say He was the *"true bread"* that came down from heaven? John 6:32-35, "Then Jesus said unto them, Verily, verily, I say unto you, Moses gave you not that bread from heaven; but my Father giveth you the true bread from heaven. For the bread of God is he which cometh down from heaven, and giveth life unto the world." Verse 34, "Then said they unto him, Lord, evermore give us this bread." Verse 35, "And Jesus said unto them, I AM THE BREAD OF LIFE: he that cometh to me shall never hunger; and he that believeth on me shall never thirst." (emphasis added).

John told us one of the reasons Jesus came, which was to destroy the works of the enemy. *I John 3:8* states, *"for this purpose the Son of God was manifested, that He might destroy the works of the devil."* Do you see? Jesus said, *"I AM THE BREAD OF LIFE."* What did He come to do? Destroy the works of the enemy!

Gideon gets revelation for the battle in the camp of the enemy! He listens to what the enemy has to say. The tents of wickedness are going to fall flat because of a *"loaf of barley bread."* The barley harvest was the *"first fruits harvest."* It means that we are included. How? What do you mean? Let the Apostle Paul declare what you are in *I Corinthians 10:17, "For we being many, are ONE BREAD and ONE BODY."* (emphasis added). We're the bread! We are the body! What body? THE BODY OF CHRIST! The body of Christ is the loaf of barley bread that destroys the works of the enemy!

Gideon the Worshipper

When Gideon heard the dream and the interpretation of it, what was his response? What did he do? My friend, Gideon was a forerunner and prototype to show us what to do in a time of fear. He WORSHIPPED!! Let God tell you unequivocally what he did (*Judges 7:15*), *"And it was so, when Gideon heard the telling of the dream and the interpretation thereof, that he WORSHIPPED"* (emphasis added). Not only do you get a "Word from God" in the enemy's camp, but you can worship there too! Can you imagine the scene? Gideon is outside the tent in the darkness, hearing the enemy's dream and interpretation. This is one definite occasion where there had to be "quiet worship," wanting to shout "Hallelujah" but having to restrain yourself. Must have been quite a worship service. At least the Presbyterians would have felt at home. Ha! (I'm really not making fun of the Presbyterians but sometimes it's just good to laugh!)

Defeating the Enemy Through Worship

Strategy as to <u>what</u> to do, how to fight the battle, <u>when</u> to engage the enemy (in this case, the Midianites, the Amalekites and the children of the east) comes as a result of worship. Really, who would choose to fight late at night? No one but a worshipper. Who would choose to fight the enemy with trumpets, candles and clay jars? No one in their right mind but a worshipper. Who would choose to fight an army of over 150,000 with just 300 men? Absurd. No one but a worshipper. When Gideon has 32,000 men, at least then he was only out manned 5 to 1. Now, it's incredible and unbelievable! Who in their right mind would go into the center of the enemy's camp and blow a <u>TRUMPET</u> to announce that you're there? A worshipper. And then break the clay jar with the candle burning to show that you're a great target? A worshipper. And, to add to the insanity of the strategy, *"SHOUT, The sword of the Lord and of Gideon."* A worshipper. Read *II Corinthians 10:3-4, 17. Verse 3, "For though we walk in the flesh* (Gideon's 300 men) *we do not war after the flesh* (don't approach the enemy on his terms, i.e. be a Spirit man, be a Spirit woman). *Verse 4, "For the weapons of our warfare are not carnal"* (swords, spears, shields*)* *"but <u>MIGHTY</u> through God to the pulling down of strongholds"* (the defeat of the enemies of our God). *Verse 17, "But he that glorieth, let him glory in the Lord."* (So our Sovereign God might receive praise, honor and glory.)

So, the question remains: who would fight at night a battle of ancient warfare, which was unheard of in Gideon's day? Answer: God would! *"The battle is not yours but God's"* (*II Chronicles 20:15*). Who would use a man to be the leader of a measly 300 men to fight overwhelming odds? God would! *"There is no restraint to the Lord to save by many or by few."* (*I Samuel 14:6*) Who would use a candle in a clay jar, a light to defeat the powers of darkness? God would! *"Ye are the light of the world"* (*Matthew 5:14*).

"The spirit of man is the candle of the Lord." (*Proverbs 20:23*) Who would use a TRUMPET and a man's SHOUT to defeat an army of 150,000 enemy troops? God would! *"No weapon that is formed against thee shall prosper."*(*Isaiah 54:17*). God will give His remnant supernatural protection.

Do you see, or rather, can you see the application of *I Thessalonians* in the story of Gideon's battle against the Midianites, Amalekites and the children of the east? When the majority of people are fearful to fight. When men and women are taught the sky is going to open when trouble hits and they're going to make a hasty exit. When apathy persists in government, and a preoccupation with futurism in eschatology continues in the pew. When materialism bombards our minds on a daily basis, then I agree we're going to interpret *I Thessalonians 4:16-17* as our escape from battle and a refusal to combat the forces of darkness. But can you perceive that perhaps the story of Gideon is truly a call to battle and not retreat? Of staying and not leaving? Of being left behind and not being "raptured?"

You may say, "Well, it's not clear. I do see the words "TRUMPET" and "SHOUT" in the story of Gideon." OK, let's go back to the text and read it (*Judges 7:19-20*). *"So Gideon, and the hundred men that were with him, came unto the outside of the camp in the beginning of the middle watch; and they had but newly set the watch: and they blew the trumpets, and broke the pitchers that were in their hands."* Verse 20, *"And the three companies blew the trumpets, and broke the pitchers, and held the lamps in their left hands, and the trumpets in their right hands to blow withal: and they cried, The sword of the Lord, and of Gideon."* In the text the word TRUMPET is pronounced. May I point out the blowing of the trumpets were not to awaken the saints! It was to awaken the ungodly that judgment was on the way! The saints were already blowing a trumpet for victory and they were getting ready to SHOUT! It says they *"CRIED, the sword of the Lord, and of Gideon."* I declare to you it wasn't a whisper, whimper or a timorous monotone. It was a "SHOUT" like the green berets or marines. It was a BATTLE CRY! That's what *I Thessalonians 4:16-17* portrays.

You may tell me, "All right, I see TRUMPET and SHOUT, but what about CAUGHT UP? I don't see it in these verses." Oh, I agree with you, it's not there in *Verse 20*, but it is in previous verses. *Judges 7:9* says, *"Arise get thee down."* Verse 10 says, *"go thou with Phurah, thy servant, down to the host."* Verse 11 goes on to say, *"and afterwards shall thine hands be strengthened to go down unto the host. Then went he down with Phurah."* I ask you, "If in 3 verses it says the enemy was "down," where would that have placed and positioned Gideon and his 300 men?" UP! That's right. CAUGHT UP! Doesn't the Word, the New Testament tell us in *Ephesians 1:3, "Blessed be the God and Father of our Lord Jesus Christ, who hath blessed us with all spiritual blessings in heavenly places in Christ."* The phrase *"in heavenly places"* literally means "in the heavenlies." We should already be CAUGHT UP! Caught up in the Spirit...caught up in victory...caught up in praise and worship!

My friend, lift up your voice like a TRUMPET and SHOUT that you've already been CAUGHT UP!

There is one last thought in the story of Gideon that portrays a glorious reality for you in a scripture in the New Testament. Who knows? Perhaps it may even get you shouting? Read *II Corinthians 4:6-7* slowly, prayerfully and worshipfully. I have no doubt that you may even be "caught up."

It's really the story of Gideon updated and it includes you. That's right – you! *Verse 6, "For God who commanded the light to shine"* (Gideon and his 300 men had candles in the jar. Rise and shine for thy light has come.) *"out of darkness"* (when did they fight the battle? in the middle of the night!) *"hath shined on our hearts"* (that's you and me; why?) *"to give the light of the knowledge of the glory of God"* (that's the victory; but where?) *"in the face of Jesus Christ." Verse 7, "But we have this treasure in earthen vessels."* What are you made of? Clay – you're the earthen vessel! What's the treasure? The light of the knowledge of God. How does it come out? ONLY BY BROKENNESS! *"That the excellency of the power may be of God and not of us."* If by "brokenness" we admit we don't have all the answers, and we haven't considered anything but what our denomination tells us to believe, and that our religious pride and prejudice must be left behind. Then and only then, we may be "CAUGHT UP" in a new reality and higher dimension. I prayerfully urge you on to brokenness!

The Price of Freedom is not Pride but Humility and Brokenness

Proud People	Broken People
Focus on the failure of others	Overwhelmed with sense of own spiritual need
"What's in it for me?"	"How can I help and bless someone?"
Look down on others	Esteem all others better then themselves
Independent - self sufficient	Have a dependent spirit - recognize the needs of others
Maintain control, "must be my way"	Surrender control
Have to prove they are right	Willing to yield the right to be right
Claim rights	Yield rights, claim duty
Demanding spirit	Giving spirit
Self protecting of rights, time, reputation	Self denying, disciplined, compassionate
Desire to be served	Motivated to serve others
Live for the moment	Live with eternity's values in view
Desire to be a success	Desire to be faithful to make others a success
Acquiring and grasping	Relinquishing success and releasing
Desire to be recognized - appreciated	Thrilled to be used at all - eager for others to get credit
Think of what they can do for God	Know that they have nothing to offer God
Feel confident in how much they know	Humbled by how much they have to learn
Self conscious	Not concerned with self at all
Keep people at arms length	Risky living, vulnerable
Quick to blame others	Accept personal responsibility, can see and admit when they are wrong
Defensive when criticized	Receive criticism with humble heart, open mind, forgiving spirit
Concerned with being respectable	Concerned with being real
Concerned about what others think	All that matters is what God knows
Compare themselves with others and feel deserving of honor	Sense the holiness of God, realize their inadequacy and the desperate need for mercy
Blind to their true heart condition	Repentant and walk in light
Don't think they have anything to repent of	Introspection within constant vigilance of a right spirit
Harbor bitterness for years	Desire to keep short accounts with God and others
Desire to be in limelight, leadership position, spotlight on them	Need no position, title, outward recognition
Fault finding	Solution seeking
External and loud	Internal and quiet
Troublemakers	Peacemakers
Disavow the authority of scripture	Always submit to the authority and spirit of the Word
Self centered	God centered

Chapter 11

"The Valley of Battle Becomes the Valley of Praise"

Let's move on to brokenness; there is a war going on. There is conflict. What will it take to win the battle for your mind? For that is really where the conflict reaches its flashpoint. Many wonderful, religious people will battle for a worthless, traditional point of view because of doctrines, personalities and concepts that are based on half-truths, or worse yet, on lies. Do we want proof? Let Isaiah declare to us just how far God's people move from truth to error. Isaiah was, in the verses you are about to read, admonishing Judah not to make alliances with Egypt. Remember now, the name Judah means 'praise'. They were God's people. How is it possible that a people of 'praise' turn to lies and trust in outright untruths? Let Isaiah tell us in *Isaiah 30:9,* *"That this is a rebellious people, lying children, children who will not hear the law of the Lord."* *Verse 10, "Which say to the seers, see not; and to the prophets, Prophecy not unto us right things* (the truth); *speak unto us smooth things, prophecy*

> **What will it take to win the battle for your mind?**

deceits." "Oh well," you say, "that's the Old Testament." What about the New Testament? Has anything changed in human personality? What was Paul's admonition to his son in the faith? He wrote to Timothy in his second letter and declared in *II Timothy 4:1-4, "I charge thee therefore before God, and the Lord Jesus Christ, who shall judge the quick and the dead at his appearing and his kingdom;" Verse 2, "Preach the word; be instant in season, out of season; reprove, rebuke, exhort with all longsuffering and doctrine." Verse 3, "For the time will come when they will not endure sound doctrine; but after their own lusts shall they heap to themselves teachers, having itching ears;" Verse 4, "And they shall turn away their ears from the truth, and shall be turned unto fables."* Notice in *Verses 1 and 2* he charged Timothy that the Lord Jesus was going to judge the quick (living) and the dead at the APPEARING (not the disappearing) of His Kingdom. Notice if you will *Verse 3, "For the time will come when they* (God's people) *will not endure sound teaching; they will go after teachers having itching ears."* (i.e. prophecy smooth things in which my tender sensibilities will be stroked, my tender ego enlarged and by all means, don't upset my escapism mentality).

Can I ask you a question to provoke you to think, to challenge you to change? Don't you find it a little bit incredulous that the church world is looking for an antichrist? Some of the main prophecy experts are trying to name one. Predictions abound; conferences on prophecy emphasize the big boogey man. Do you realize this emphasis is <u>NOT</u> a Biblical perspective?

The purpose of prophecy IS TO REVEAL THE NATURE OF GOD and HIS HOLINESS! *Acts 10:43, "<u>TO HIM</u>"* (not the devil, not the dragon, not the beast, not the antichrist) *but <u>TO HIM</u> (Jesus) give <u>all</u> the <u>prophets</u> <u>witness</u> that through His NAME, whosoever believeth in Him shall receive remission of sins."*

The ultimate intention of prophecy is to give testimony to the Son of God. Sure, prophecy is also given to warn God's people, to admonish nations, to caution God's people concerning approaching evil. However, let the scriptures be the <u>final</u> authority! Read aloud *Revelation 19:9-10, "...and he saith unto me, These are the <u>TRUE SAYINGS OF GOD</u>."* (emphasis added) *Verse 10, "And I fell at his feet to worship him. And he said unto me, See thou do it not: I am thy fellow servant and of thy brethren that have the <u>testimony of Jesus</u>: Worship God: for the TESTIMONY of JESUS <u>IS THE</u> SPIRIT OF PROPHECY."* It cannot get any plainer than that! The focus of prophecy is <u>CHRIST</u> – not the antichrist! The centrality is always Jesus! Jesus – first, foremost and final!

The Psalmist David cried out long ago in *Psalms 34:3, "Oh, magnify the Lord with me and <u>LET US</u> exalt His name together."* By the way, how do you magnify the Lord? How do you make Him bigger? Is it possible? How do you enlarge Him who fills the universe? The answer: the only way He can be magnified is to become bigger in your mind, in your understanding, in your comprehension and in your heart. Get closer to Him and He'll get bigger. How big is He to you? Is He bigger than the antichrist? The C.F.R.? The Illuminati? The conspiracies? Your denomination? If He isn't, then your focus is like King Saul and the armies of Israel in the day of battle with the Philistines. We'll all get out our tape measures and begin to magnify Goliath. As we shrink back in fear and shriek out in terror, "Look how BIG our enemy is," do you comprehend what we're doing? We're aggrandizing our enemy; he gets bigger and bigger. We're actually magnifying the devil's crowd. Don't you get tired of hearing how big the devil is?

I guarantee in David's day that from God's viewpoint and from heaven's perspective, Goliath was <u>NOT</u> the giant. From God's vantage point, David the stripling, David the shepherd boy, David the teenager was the GIANT! In this hour of extremity, in this day when the situation is serious and the saints are not, God is still developing David(s). He is still making a "manchild ministry" in the hearts of praisers and worshippers. Nothing else really is of any consequence to our God.

Have you come to the place where you have no strength, where you don't know what to do? When you're outnumbered or surrounded, then let the "valley of battle" become the "Valley of Praise." Let's take a journey in scripture to find out how our Heavenly Father used a choir of praisers to rout an antichrist army.

Let's look at the army that God chooses. I've heard of church splits because of jealousy amongst the choir director and the organist, the pastor and the pianist, the jockeying for position because of talent, excellence of musical ability and professionalism. The bottom line of God's criteria for His choir is <u>NOT HOW</u> you sing but <u>WHY</u> you sing. Also, WHEN you sing – in the face of adversity. The following text tells the story of a choir <u>FIGHT</u> that I would like to get in on. If you thought the story of Gideon breaking jars, letting the light shine, shouting and blowing the trumpets was a hoot, then this episode in the annals of warfare is hilarious. I know God laughs because the Word says He does! *Psalms 2:4* declares, *"He who sitteth in the heavens shall laugh…"* I'm quite sure in the text you're about to read that God was grinning and even chuckling about the thought that the choir was going to be His "assault team." Talk about "special forces." We're about to experience worship warfare.

This is how God and His people win battles. Read the following text in *II Chronicles 20:1, 3-22, 25-29, "It came to pass after this also, that the children of Moab, and the children of Ammon, and with them other beside the Ammonites, came against Jehoshaphat to battle." Verse 3, "And Jehoshaphat feared, and set himself to seek the Lord, and proclaimed a fast throughout all Judah." Verse 4, "And Judah gathered themselves together, to ask help of the Lord: even out of all the cities of Judah they came to seek the Lord." Verse 5, "And Jehoshaphat stood in the congregation of Judah and Jerusalem, in the house of the Lord, before the new court," Verse 6, "And said, O Lord God of our fathers, art not thou God in heaven? And rulest not thou over all the kingdoms of the heathen? And in thine hand is there not power and might, so that none is able to withstand thee?" Verse 7, "Art not thou our God, who didst drive out the inhabitants of this land before thy people Israel, and gavest it to the seed of Abraham thy friend forever?" Verse 8, "And they dwelt therein, and have built thee a sanctuary therein for thy name, saying," Verse 9, "If, when evil cometh upon us as the sword, judgment, or pestilence, or famine, we stand before this house, and in thy presence, (for thy name is in this house) and cry unto thee in our affliction, then thou wilt hear and help." Verse 10, "And now, behold, the children of Ammon and Moab and mount Seir, whom thou wouldest not let Israel invade, when they came out of the land of Egypt, but they turned from them, and destroyed them not;" Verse 11, "Behold, I say, how they reward us, to come to cast us out of thy possession, which thou hast given us to inherit." Verse 12, "O our God, wilt thou not judge them? For we have no might against this great company that cometh against us; neither know we what to do: but our eyes are upon thee." Verse 13, "And all Judah stood before the Lord, with their little ones, their wives, and their children." Verse 14, "Then upon Jahaziel the son of Zechariah, the son of Benaiah, the son of Jeiel, the son of Mattaniah, a Levite of the sons of Asaph, came the Spirit of the Lord in the midst of the congregation;" Verse 15, "And he said, Hearken ye, all Judah, and ye inhabitants of Jerusalem, and thou king Jehoshaphat, Thus saith the Lord unto you, Be not afraid nor dismayed by reason of this great multitude; for the battle is not yours, but God's." Verse 16, "Tomorrow go ye down against them: behold, they come up by the cliff of Ziz; and ye shall find them at the end of the brook, before the wilderness of Jeruel." Verse 17, "Ye shall not need to fight in this battle: set yourselves, stand ye still, and see the salvation of the Lord with you, O Judah and Jerusalem: fear not, nor be dismayed; tomorrow go out against them: for the Lord will be with you." Verse 18, "And Jehoshaphat bowed his head with his face to the ground: and all Judah and the inhabitants of Jerusalem fell before the Lord, worshipping the Lord." Verse 19, "And the Levites, of the children of the Kohathites, and of the children of the Korhites, stood up to praise the Lord God of Israel with a loud voice on high." Verse 20, "And they rose early in the morning, and went forth into the wilderness of Tekoa: and as they went forth, Jehoshaphat stood and said, Hear me, O Judah, and ye inhabitants of Jerusalem; Believe in the Lord your God, so shall ye be established, believe his prophets, so shall ye prosper." Verse 21, "And when he had consulted with the people, he appointed singers unto the Lord, and that should praise the beauty of holiness, as they went out before the army, and to say, Praise the Lord; for his mercy endureth forever." Verse 22, "And when they began to sing and to praise, the Lord set ambushments against the children of Ammon, Moab, and mount Seir, which were come against Judah: and they were smitten." Verse 25, "And when Jehoshaphat and his people came to take away the spoil of them, they found among them in abundance both riches with the dead bodies, and precious jewels, which they stripped off for themselves, more than they could carry away: and they were three days in gathering of the spoil, it was so much." Verse 26, "And on the fourth day they assembled themselves in the valley of Berachah; for there they blessed the Lord: therefore the name of the same place was called, The valley of Berachah, unto this day." Verse 27, "Then they returned, every man of Judah and Jerusalem, and Jehoshaphat in the forefront of them, to go again to Jerusalem with joy; for the Lord had made them to rejoice over their enemies." Verse 28, "And they came to Jerusalem with psalteries and harps and trumpets unto the house of the Lord." Verse 29, "And the fear of God was on all the kingdoms of those countries, when they had heard that the Lord fought against the enemies of Israel."*

Can you believe this story? Isn't it marvelous the King of Judah in the *Verses 5-11* reminds our Heavenly Father what He has done in the past. He rehearses and reiterates the history of God's faithfulness. Jehoshaphat does NOT give credit to the enemies of God.

If all we see in this day is disaster, devastation, doom and dissolution, we will not be able to see brighter days ahead. I checked the owner's manual. The best is yet to be. Our God is able. He will do exceedingly, abundantly above that we are able to even ask or think. I have news for the tares, for the evildoers, for the antichrists, for the one-world-globalists: the Kingdom of God is not looking at its last hour of life.

We're not taking refuge in a vote of spineless politicians, preachers, or profiteers whose future is as bankrupt as their sense of destiny. We choose not to embrace a fatalistic view of the future or our Father's plan. The best is yet to be. It's been said, "It's not over till the fat lady sings." We've got one better. It's not over till the CHOIR sings – God's choir. And it is not sometime in the future, "When the roll is called up yonder." Why not give Him praise right now?

With the battle about to be set in array, King Jehoshaphat gathers the people and makes admissions that are unheard of in the political realm. The first is *Verse 12, "we have no might."* The second admission was *"neither know we what to do."* Wouldn't it really be refreshing to hear our President declare on a national TV and radio broadcast, "We are not going to rely on any army, navy or air force for we have no military might. Furthermore no one in the executive, legislative or judicial branch of government knows what to do. So we are going to look to the covenant-keeping God of Abraham, Isaac and Jacob. Our eyes are solely going to look to Him for protection, preservation and defense. We, as a nation are going to station ourselves with the Captain of all ages."

Who Initiates Revival?

Do you understand in Biblical history when a revival of spirituality swept across the land, it was not because of the priests (preachers) but because of the kings (civil government)? Go ahead; check it out! Kings would call for a fast. *II Chronicles 20:3, "And Jehoshaphat feared, and set himself to seek the Lord, and proclaimed a fast throughout all Judah." Jeremiah 36:9, "And it came to pass in the fifth year of Jehoiakim the son of Josiah king of Judah, in the ninth month, that they proclaimed a fast before the Lord to all the people in Jerusalem, and to all the people that came from the cities of Judah unto Jerusalem." Jonah 3:5, "So the people of Nineveh believed God, and proclaimed a fast, and put on sackcloth, from the greatest of them even to the least of them."*

God would answer with revival and restoration. How? God would send a prophet! Are you ready to hear what God has to say? The prophet declared in *II Chronicles 20:16, "Tomorrow <u>GO YE DOWN</u>* (emphasis added) *against them* (the enemy).*"* If the admonition is GO YE DOWN, then where were they? Could it be that they were "CAUGHT UP?" The prophetic decree that followed was "Don't fear, don't be dismayed, don't be afraid, this isn't your battle, it belongs to God and He knows how to fight!" Your part is to sing, praise and worship. But we say, "Oh, we'll leave that up to the angels or the women." Our macho manhood and muscle bound bravado declares, "I'll fight the battle and give the spoils of victory to God." But He in His inimitable wisdom whispers, "I'll tell you what: you sing, I'll fight and I'll give you the spoils of battle." Don't you like His arrangement better? *Verse 18* declares the King and the people *"fell before the Lord worshipping the Lord."* We have a choice: we can

> **If you win in worship, the battle is a piece of cake.**

either fall before the Lord in worship or fall before our enemies in defeat. You see, the real battle is waged in worship. Haven't we heard it said, "Before you go into battle, pray." No, my friend, prayer is the battle! Worship is the defining element of victory. No worship – no victory. If you win in worship, the battle is a piece of cake.

Let's look and see if in this battle we can find "SHOUT" and "TRUMPET." *Verse 19* says, *"God's people stood up to praise the Lord God of Israel with a LOUD VOICE (SHOUT) on high."* (emphasis added) Doesn't this chapter have the ingredients of *I Thessalonians 4:16-18* involved in it? *Verse 28* states, *"And they came to Jerusalem with psalteries and harps and "TRUMPETS"* (emphasis added) *unto the house of the Lord."* Again we see in this chapter a call to BATTLE, a call to involvement and commitment. Truly we affirm, *"It's not by might* (military might), *it's not by power* (political power), *<u>BUT BY MY SPIRIT</u> saith the Lord!"* (*Zechariah 4:6*) (emphasis added).

Could it be in our day of technology and mechanized sophistication, that we would be able to sing and praise our way to deliverance? Long before we developed stinger missiles and "smart" bombs guided to their targets by laser beams, our God made "smart" "HAILSTONES" (*Exodus 9:22, 25-26*), *"And the Lord said unto Moses, Stretch forth thine hand toward heaven that there may be hail in all the land of Egypt, upon man, and upon beast and upon every herb of the field." Verse 25, "And the hail smote throughout all the land of Egypt all that were in the field, both man and beast and the hail smote every herb of the field and broke every tree of the field." Verse 26, "Only in the land of Goshen, where the children of Israel were, was there no hail."* Do you think that our Mighty God and King has forgotten how to protect you in the midst of tribulation? Can He still rain down manna from heaven to feed a nation for 40 years? What makes us think that He can't get water out of a rock in the 21st century? Miracles are the signature of God throughout history. Do you think He's forgotten how to write His name?

Did He or did He not get Paul and Silas out of jail in Philippi? Let the record tell us how. They didn't have to appeal to an earthly court for judicial review or get a lawyer from the legal defense team. They didn't submit a writ of "habeas corpus" or file a brief. They did what Jehoshaphat did with the choir 600 years before. They prayed and they sang! *Acts 16:25-26, "And at midnight* (when it's hardest to sing) *Paul and Silas PRAYED and SANG* (emphasis added) *praises unto God, and the prisoners heard them."* So, then what happened? *Verse 26, "And SUDDENLY there was a great earthquake so that the foundations of the prison were shaken; and IMMEDIATELY* (emphasis added) *all the doors were opened, and everyone's bands were loosed."* I even found out the name of that prison in Philippi. It was Sing Sing.

Do you think deliverance would have come if they were mumbling, grumbling and finding fault and complaining? Not a chance! My next question deserves an honest answer from you. Would they have had just cause to complain to God about the way they were being treated? More than likely, yes. Were they criminals? No! Did they get a "beating" for doing something good? Yes. What was the reason they had their clothes ripped off and the lash cut deep in the tender flesh of their backs? Answer: they cast out a spirit of divination (Greek-python) from a young girl. Did God "rapture" them out of their circumstances? No! Did they go through tribulation? Yes! Why did they have to go THROUGH this terrible humiliation and pain? Answer: to get the sheriff (the jailer) and his family saved! *Acts 16:30-34, "And brought them out, and said, Sirs, what must I do to be saved?" Verse 31, "And they said, Believe on the Lord Jesus Christ, and thou shalt be saved, and thy house." Verse 32, "And they spake unto him the word of the Lord, and to all that were in his house." Verse 33, "And he took them the same hour of the night, and washed their stripes; and was baptized, he and all his house, straightway." Verse 34, "And when he had brought them into his house, he set meat before them, and rejoiced, believing in God with all his house."* God in His magnificent and awesome wisdom knew the only way to get Paul and Silas to meet the jailer was to provide the difficult circumstances (negative ones, at that) to facilitate that acquaintance. When you see Paul and Silas, ask them if the beating was worth the salvation of the jailer and his family. They will answer, "Yes, a thousand times - yes!"

Some things in life are really incongruous and antithetical? You ask, "What do you mean?" Simply this: we sing choruses like "Gimee that ol' time religion, gimme that ol' time religion, gimme that ol' time religion…it's good enough for me." And then we come to the verse and warble, "It was good for Paul and Silas, it was good for Paul and Silas, it was good for Paul and Silas…and it's good enough <u>FOR ME</u>!"

Who are we kidding? We don't want the kind that will get us in trouble with the authorities. Why, we're respectable! Give me my soft cushioned pew, my lush, plush, lavish air-conditioned foxhole. Give me a status-seeking stained glass sanctuary replete with a "Christian" humanistic professional seminarian that can tell me how good I am.

The "god" that is presented on television week to week (no, weak to weak) is an inoffensive, loving, lifeless, jello cosmic force. Why, this innocuous, serviceable deity gathers all religions around the banner of the United Nations as we parade to religious services arm in arm with the Rabbi, Father, Bhagwam, Bhuddist, Hindu, Mufti Muslim clerics. Give me a very large break! Our Savior, Jesus Christ the Lord is God! He has no equal! He is incomparable! He is God alone and He alone is worthy of praise. Away with this nauseating quasi-religious junk!

Let's get back to SHOUT, TRUMPET and CAUGHT UP in God's Word. *II Chronicles 20:20-21, "And they rose early in the morning, and went forth into the wilderness of Tekoa: and as they went forth, Jehoshaphat stood and said, Hear me, O Judah, and ye inhabitants of Jerusalem; Believe in the Lord your God, so shall ye be established; believe his prophets, so shall ye prosper." Verse 21, "And when he had consulted with the people, he appointed singers unto the Lord, and that should praise the beauty of holiness, as they went out before the army, and to say, Praise the Lord; for his mercy endureth forever."* What kind of eyesight is desired when you go to an optometrist? Isn't it called 20/20 vision? If you want perfect spiritual vision, memorize the last half of *Verse 20, "Believe the Lord your God, so shall ye be established, believe His prophets so shall ye prosper."* My friend, it doesn't say believe in the "<u>rapture</u>." It says believe in the Lord your God and the prophets. Did they say anything about the "rapture?" No! It's a man-made term.

You may be getting the feeling that I'm myopic about this subject and my whole emphasis in ministry is trying to disprove this teaching. I assure you I have no lifetime crusade of bashing a word that is not even found in your Bible. I just see that its acceptance in the church has emasculated its power and neutered its effectiveness. You might ask me, "Ron, would you <u>like</u> to believe in a "rapture?" My answer: SURE, but I just don't find any scriptural support in the Bible. You see, dear friend, at one time I was a proponent of the any moment "snatch." But one day I put away the popular best sellers in Christian bookstores and got in the BOOK. And you know what? The BOOK got in me. I've been spoiled! If this small compilation of historical facts along with scripture gets you back to the BOOK, the BIBLE, then I will say, "mission accomplished!"

One last thought: when Jehoshaphat consulted with the people and appointed singers to go into battle with the army, do you know what song they sang? Want to guess? Here's a hint. The title is in the last portion of *Verse 21: "Praise the Lord for His mercy endureth forever."* Go ahead; turn in your Biblical songbook to page 136 or rather, *Psalm 136*. This is the song they sang 2,600 years ago to make the "valley of battle" the "valley of praise." Sing it, get <u>caught up</u> and <u>shout,</u> for each verse ends with *"FOR HIS MERCY ENDURETH FOREVER."*(emphasis added).

Psalms 136:1-26, "O give thanks unto the Lord; for He is good: FOR HIS MERCY ENDURETH FOREVER." Verse 2, "O give thanks unto the God of gods: FOR HIS MERCY ENDURETH FOREVER." Verse 3, "O give thanks to the Lord of lords: FOR HIS MERCY ENDURETH FOREVER." Verse 4, "To him who alone doeth great wonders: FOR HIS MERCY ENDURETH FOREVER." Verse 5, "To Him that by wisdom made the heavens: FOR HIS MERCY ENDURETH FOREVER." Verse 6, "To him that stretched out the earth above the waters: FOR HIS MERCY ENDURETH FOREVER." Verse 7, "To him that made great lights: FOR HIS MERCY ENDURETH FOREVER." Verse 8, "The sun to rule by day: FOR HIS MERCY ENDURETH FOREVER." Verse 9, "The moon and stars to rule by night: FOR HIS MERCY ENDURETH FOREVER." Verse 10, "To him that smote Egypt in their firstborn: FOR HIS MERCY ENDURETH FOREVER." Verse 11, "And brought out Israel from among them: FOR HIS MERCY ENDURETH FOREVER." Verse 12, "With a strong hand, and with a stretched out arm: FOR HIS MERCY ENDURETH FOREVER." Verse 13, "To him which divided the Red Sea into parts: FOR HIS MERCY ENDURETH FOREVER." Verse 14, "And made Israel to pass through the midst of it: FOR HIS MERCY ENDURETH FOREVER." Verse15, "But overthrew Pharaoh and his host in the Red Sea: FOR HIS MERCY ENDURETH FOREVER." Verse 16, "To him which led his people through the wilderness: FOR HIS MERCY ENDURETH FOREVER." Verse 17, "To him which smote great kings: FOR HIS MERCY ENDURETH FOREVER:"

Verse 18, "And slew famous kings: FOR HIS MERCY ENDURETH FOREVER:" Verse 19, "Sihon king of the Amorites: FOR HIS MERCY ENDURETH FOREVER:" Verse 20, "And Og the king of Bashan: FOR HIS MERCY ENDURETH FOREVER:" Verse 21, "And gave their land for a heritage: and HIS MERCY ENDURETH FOREVER:" Verse 22, "Even a heritage unto Israel his servant: FOR HIS MERCY ENDURETH FOREVER." Verse 23, "Who remembered us in our low estate: FOR HIS MERCY ENDURETH FOREVER:" Verse 24, "And hath redeemed us from our enemies: FOR HIS MERCY ENDURETH FOREVER." Verse 25, "Who giveth food to all flesh: FOR HIS MERCY ENDURETH FOREVER." Verse 26, "O give thanks unto the God of heaven: FOR HIS MERCY ENDURETH FOREVER." (emphasis added).

All the elements of *I Thessalonians 4:16-17* are found in the story of the *"valley of praise."* SHOUT, TRUMPET, CAUGHT UP! His mercy still endures – for you, and for me. For that, we worship Him in unending praise and adoration.

Chapter 12

Solomon's Temple Dedicated

SHOUT, TRUMPET, CAUGHT UP

Every event in God's Word holds an important lesson for us, upon whom *"the ends of the age have come."* (See *I Corinthians 10:11*) The unfolding event of a phenomenal display of God's manifested glory is recorded in the dedication of Solomon's temple. Read the account in *II Chronicles 5:1-14* and picture the scene.

II Chronicles 5:1-14, "Thus all the work that Solomon made for the house of the LORD was finished: and Solomon brought in all the things that David his father had dedicated; and the silver, and the gold, and all the instruments, put he among the treasures of the house of God." Verse 2, "Then Solomon assembled the elders of Israel, and all the heads of the tribes, the chief of the fathers of the children of Israel, unto Jerusalem, to bring up the ark of the covenant of the LORD out of the city of David, which is Zion." Verse 3, "Wherefore all the men of Israel assembled themselves unto the king in the feast which was in the seventh month." Verse 4 "And all the elders of Israel came; and the Levites took up the ark. Verse 5, "And they brought up the ark, and the tabernacle of the congregation, and all the holy vessels that were in the tabernacle, these did the priests and the Levites bring up. Verse 6, "Also king Solomon, and all the congregation of Israel that were assembled unto him before the ark, sacrificed sheep and oxen, which could not be told nor numbered for multitude." Verse 7, "And the priests brought in the ark of the covenant of the LORD unto his place, to the oracle of the house, into the most holy place, even under the wings of the cherubim:" Verse 8, "For the cherubim spread forth their wings over the place of the ark, and the cherubim covered the ark and the staves thereof above." Verse 9, "And they drew out the staves of the ark, that the ends of the staves were seen from the ark before the oracle; but they were not seen without. And there it is unto this day." Verse 10, "There was nothing in the ark save the two tables which Moses put therein at Horeb, when the LORD made a covenant with the children of Israel, when they came out of Egypt." Verse 11, "And it came to pass, when the priests were come out of the holy place: (for all the priests that were present were sanctified, and did not then wait by course:" Verse 12, "Also the Levites which were the singers, all of them of Asaph, of Heman, of Jeduthun, with their sons and their brethren, being arrayed in white linen, having cymbals and psalteries and harps, stood at the east end of the altar, and with them a hundred and twenty priests sounding with trumpets:" Verse 13, "It came even to pass, as the trumpeters and singers were as one, to make one sound to be heard in praising and thanking the LORD; and when they lifted up their voice with the trumpets and cymbals and instruments of music, and praised the LORD, saying, For he is good; for his mercy endureth forever: that then the house was filled with a cloud, even the house of the LORD;" Verse 14, "So that the priests could not stand to minister by reason of the cloud: for the glory of the LORD had filled the house of God."

As you can see by the story, this is a picture of the coming of the Lord to His temple. Verse one tells us the work was finished and completed. The scaffolding had come down; litter and debris had been removed. Work and labor had ceased. The dedication was about to begin. Dignitaries from all the tribes of had arrived. Musicians and singers were awaiting their turn to participate in an event that took decades to prepare for. The day had finally arrived with an air of excitement and expectancy. Aren't you going to be glad when the work is completed with you?

> **But the truth is…God always has something MORE.**

Is it essential for you to notice the month in which the dedication of this temple takes place. *Verse 3* declares, *"Wherefore all the men of Israel assembled themselves unto the king in the feast which was in the seventh month."* Does the <u>seventh</u> mean anything to us? Is there anything significant about the <u>seventh</u> month that should capture our attention?

Let's ask ourselves a few questions. How many times a year did God require His people to assemble in special convocation before Him in the Old Testament? *Exodus 34:23* say, *"Thrice in the year shall your male children (son ship) appear before the Lord God, the God of Israel."*
(For a detailed account read *Leviticus 23:4-44*)

Let's list those three times Israel was to appear before their God.
  1) Passover
  2) Pentecost
  3) Tabernacles

Has Passover been fulfilled? Why sure, you say. Jesus is our Passover Lamb and that feast has been fulfilled in its' entirety.

Well what about Pentecost, which took place fifty days later? We hear so many teachers and preachers telling us we need to go back and celebrate Pentecost. My friend, do you realize the feast of Pentecost was already fulfilled about 2,000 years ago? Let the scriptural record declare to us this important fact. *Acts 2:1* says, *"And when the day of Pentecost was <u>FULLY</u>*

come, they were all with one accord in one place. " God is not going around in circles. That feast had already *"fully"* come. Peter got up that momentous day and said in effect, "This is it! This is what the prophet Joel was talking about! It's here! Pentecost has arrived in biblical fulfillment!"

Acts 2:16-21, "But this is that which was spoken by the prophet Joel;" Verse 17, "And it shall come to pass in the last days, saith God, I will pour out of my Spirit upon all flesh: and your sons and your daughters shall prophesy, and your young men shall see visions, and your old men shall dream dreams:" Verse 18, "And on my servants and on my handmaidens I will pour out in those days of my Spirit; and they shall prophesy:" Verse 19, "And I will show wonders in heaven above, and signs in the earth beneath; blood, and fire, and vapor of smoke:" Verse 20, "The sun shall be turned into darkness, and the moon into blood, before that great and notable day of the Lord come:" Verse 21, "And it shall come to pass, that whosoever shall call on the name of the Lord shall be saved.

Do I mean that Pentecost has no further significance for us to experience? No, not at all. It is an experience, not a denomination. But today when you exclaim, "Let's move on to the seventh month feast," people look at you scratching their heads in bewilderment. In reality they incredulously ask, "What in the world are you talking about?"

Some of God's people see no further than Passover. They in effect say, "I got it all in one trip to the altar. The blood of the Passover Lamb is enough for me! That's all that I care to believe."

If you share with them the experience of Pentecost and the infilling and baptism of the Holy Spirit many of them say, "I'm quite satisfied just to be 'saved.' My sins are forgiven and I'm on my way to heaven." Not knowing that there is more, or perhaps knowing, but fearful to get into something weird and extreme. But the truth is…God always has something <u>MORE</u>. No, not extra-biblical, just something more. *John 3:34* says, *"For he whom God hath sent speaketh the words of God, for God giveth not the Spirit by measure unto Him. "* God always has more.

As we look further in this dedication of Solomon's temple is it possible for us to see in miniature the *"Coming of the Lord"* to a people that had prepared themselves in measure for an appearance of the glory of the Lord? And isn't that what you're desirous of?

I was admonished and advised by professionals in the publishing business that religious people do not want to read anything that contradicts their popular pre-tribulation rapture beliefs. The prevailing philosophy of the future is shallow, puny and paltry because we've been raised on television instead of God's solid scriptural principles. We're spoiled, demanding argumentative and short-tempered. And so we've lost balance. God's people whine, complain, and find fault so easy. Somehow we've lost the understanding that God has so much more than what we presently possess. We've also lost the understanding that virtuous study is its' own reward. The real purpose of this study is to get you, dear friend, to confront yourself. Are you so sure your belief system about eschatology is foolproof?

As we look into what happened in this seventh month tabernacle experience in *II Chronicles 5*, let's see if the words SHOUT, TRUMPET and CAUGHT UP are evidenced in the text...

> *Verse 2* states *"to bring UP the ark of the covenant of the Lord..."*
>
> *Verse 3* tells us that this event takes place in the seventh month.
>
> *Verse 4* tells us *"the Levites TOOK UP the ark."*
>
> ****Interesting to note that the seventh month feast has never been fulfilled prophetically in History, meaning – there's something on God's agenda that has yet to take place***
>
> *Verse 5* states *"...they BROUGHT UP the ark..."*
>
> *Verse 12* declares that they were arrayed in white linen, which in
>
> *Revelation 19:8* reveals *"...fine linen is the righteousness of saints"* and it even tells the number of priests sounding <u>TRUMPETS</u>.

There were 120 priests sounding the trumpet message of the dedication of Solomon's temple. But even more wonderful than that temple, which was so costly, ornate, and aesthetically beautiful beyond description was the New Testament temple that was also dedicated about 2,000 years ago. It also had 120 trumpeters blowing the message of the dedication of a temple made of living stones. *Acts 1:15* says, *"And in those days Peter stood up in the midst of the disciples, and said (the number of names together was about an hundred and twenty)."* Amazing, isn't it?

In Solomon's temple it states in *II Chronicles 5:13*, *"It came even to pass, as the trumpeters and singers were as <u>one</u> to make <u>one</u> sound to be heard and praising and thanking the Lord, and when they lifted up their <u>VOICE</u>...* (SHOUT)." (emphasis added).

In the book of *Acts 2:1* it states, *"...that they were all in <u>one</u> place and in <u>one</u> accord...then the Holy Spirit came <u>down</u> and filled them <u>all</u>."* There must have been quite a bit of noise that day for 3,000 heard the message and entered into the Kingdom of God by repentance, water baptism, and being filled with the Holy Spirit.

Doesn't *I Thessalonians 4:17* say, *"Then we who are alive and remain shall be CAUGHT UP together with them in the CLOUDS to meet the Lord in the air and so shall we ever be with the Lord"*.

As we close this last paragraph look at the last half of *Verse 13 and 14* of *II Chronicles 5*, *"...and praised the Lord saying, for He is good; for His mercy endureth forever...that then the house was filled with a CLOUD even the house of the Lord... Verse 14, "So that the priests could not stand to minister by reason of the cloud; for the GLORY OF THE LORD HAD FILLED THE HOUSE OF GOD. "*(emphasis added). This is what will happen at the coming of the Lord. Our bodies, which are the temples of the living God, will be changed. It happens in <u>oneness</u>. It happens in <u>unity</u>. It <u>will</u> happen in the feast of tabernacles. Who knows? Maybe this year.

Chapter 13

The Catching Up In The Book Of Revelation

John the Beloved" – The Revelation of Jesus Christ

"SHOUT – TRUMPET – CAUGHT UP"

The powerful message of the last book of the Bible is <u>NOT</u> the Revelation of antichrist but the REVELATION of JESUS CHRIST. Why in the name of justice and righteousness is there not an outcry from the congregations throughout the land for pastors to emphasize Jesus instead of the dragon and false prophet, etc.? *Revelation 1:1* begins with *"The Revelation* (unveiling) *of Jesus Christ which God gave unto him to show* (reveal*) unto His servants things which must shortly come to pass; and He sent and signified* (written in symbolic language) *it by His angel unto His servant John."*

Church folks should question their pastors and teachers about this. I must ask you a question and it is an important one: how is it, that we are told by prophecy experts (so called) to interpret the book of *Revelation* literally when the scripture <u>clearly</u> says it was written <u>symbolically</u>? Yet, we <u>spiritualize</u> major portions of God's Word that <u>are</u> meant to be taken literally. But they say, "Oh, you must interpret "the Apocalypse" literally. Oh, really? What about the harlot in the *17th Chapter*, of which it is said in Verse 16, *"And the ten horns which thou sawest upon the beast, these shall hate the whore and shall make her desolate and naked and SHALL EAT HER FLESH* (emphasis added) *and burn her with fire."*

> **I'm not trying to avoid getting the "tattoo." I'm trying to get rid of it!**

Is this to be taken literally? Or what about the horrifying "MARK of the BEAST?" <u>In</u> your forehead or <u>in</u> your hand. Notice it doesn't say <u>ON</u> the forehead or <u>ON</u> the hand. OK, let's quote the verse that deals with the "mark of the beast."

Revelation 14:9, "And the third angel followed them, saying with a loud voice; If any man worship the beast and his image and receive his mark <u>in</u> his forehead, or <u>in</u> his hand." Sorry, I'm not buying into the computer chip deal or the "666" hysteria. There are so many laughable interpretations of taking the "brand" of the antichrist. I'm not trying to avoid getting the "tattoo." I'm trying to <u>get rid of it</u>! We've all been marked by the "beast system." Oh yes, I know the protests, hue and cry from well meaning people when they exclaim, "But you won't be able to buy or sell without the mark of the beast!" My friend, I've got news for you – you can't do that <u>NOW</u>; whether using cash, credit card or check – everything has a number on it. Go ahead; look at currency or checks or your credit cards. All are numbered: automobile VIN number; house deed numbered at the court house; tax number; social security number; phone number; airplane travel or flight number; appliances in your house; driver's license number; birth certificate number; death certificate number; from the cradle to the grave; and you're worried about "666" and the "futurist" interpretation of Revelation. Forget it!

Our God has been involved in <u>marking</u> His people from time immemorial. Way back in Ezekiel's day in *Chapter 9:3-4* the scripture says, *"And the glory of the God of Israel was gone up from the cherub upon which he was, to the threshold of the house. And he called to the man clothed with linen* (linen = righteousness – *Revelation 19:8) who had the writer's inkhorn by his side," Verse 4, "And the Lord said unto him, Go through the midst of the city, through the midst of Jerusalem and set a <u>MARK UPON THE FOREHEADS</u>* (emphasis added) *of the men that sigh and that cry for all the abominations that are done in the midst of it."* Do you get it? Do you see and understand that 2,600 years ago in Ezekiel's day that our God (not the devil), but our God, was marking (selecting and choosing out beforehand) His people? Our concern should be that we're marked by God and not the devil.

If people ask me if I'm concerned or worried about getting the "mark of the beast," my reply is "Sorry, but there's just no room in my forehead for I've got my Father's Name "<u>IN MY MIND</u>." I have developed a "Christian World View." By His <u>Grace</u>, my thinking is dominated by scripture, by His Word. I view situations through the lens of "this is my Father's World." Can you see that this is your helmet of salvation (the mind of Christ)? Forget conspiracy theories – they never saved a soul and they never will! (But, they will sell a lot of books.)

Paul the Apostle told us in 60 A.D when he wrote to the *Ephesians* church in *Chapter 1:12-14, "That we should be to the praise of His glory who first trusted in Christ." Verse 13, "In whom ye also trusted, after you heard the word of truth, the gospel of your salvation; in whom also after that ye believed, ye were <u>SEALED</u>* (marked) *with that Holy Spirit of promise." Verse 14, "Who is the earnest* (down payment*) of our inheritance, until the redemption of the purchased possession unto the praise of His glory."* Hallelujah! You've been marked by the Father of glory! Where? <u>In your mind</u>! That's why Paul told the church at Philippi, *"Let this mind be in you which was also in Christ Jesus." (Philippians 2:5)*

So, please don't worry about them inserting a computer chip under your skin so while at the check-out line in the grocery store, you'll be able to buy oatmeal, corn bread and grits. It's not a future happening. The beast system is in the here and now – it is all around us. We've all been marked in our thinking. The kingdom of darkness is here but so is the Kingdom of Light! We hear so much of the 6 million Jews. It's in news media on a daily basis. My question would be: what about the 30 million Russian Christians killed under Lenin and Stalin? Just a shrug of the shoulders – so what? Or how about the 50 million Chinese purged under Mao Tse Tung? Now, that's what I call a beast system! What's happening today against Christians in Muslim nations is horrifying beyond description. Yet we in the West buy into fictitious futurism, which declares: "Well, thank God, we won't be here; we will have been raptured."

Questions to ask yourself:

- Am I going to let others fight the battles for survival and freedom and I cop out?
- Am I going to bow my knee to corporate materialism-socialism or bow to Jesus Christ?
- Am I going to defer to the liberal ruling elite and sell my mind to the highest bidder?

Sorry, my answer is: NOT FOR SALE!
(Joshua 24:15) "As for me and my house we will serve the Lord!"

I won't shamefully compromise and sacrifice truth for political or religious expediency. Compromise's first cousin is cowardice and compromise's kissing cousin is selfishness. Those are two relatives I disown, denounce and dislike.

Before we look at SHOUT, TRUMPET and CAUGHT UP in the Biblical narrative of Revelation, let me quote a secular prophet of our day who lived under the grinding heel of totalitarianism. Because he was such a political "hot potato" they couldn't kill him so they sent him into exile. They told him, "GET OUT!!! LEAVE!" Religious organizations do the same thing today. If you disagree with prescribed "doctrinal correctness," you will be disfellowshipped, debunked, defrocked and disgraced. You'll be kicked off radio, TV and put out of the pulpit.

A Secular Prophet Speaks

Read what Alexandr Solzhenitsyn said way back in 1975. I quote, "Today there are two major processes occurring in the world. One has been in progress more than 30 years. It is a process of shortsighted concessions. A process of giving up in hope that in some point the wolf will have eaten enough. The second process is one which I consider key to everything. Under the cast-iron shell of Communism in the Soviet Union and in other Communist countries, there is a liberation of the human spirit. A new generation is growing up, one which is steadfast in its struggle with evil, one which is not willing to accept unprincipled compromises, which prefers to lose everything – life, salary, conditions of life, conditions of existence – but is not willing to sacrifice its conscience in making deals with evil." (end of quote).

I believe there is a new generation growing - a Joshua generation, a Caleb generation - that says, "I'm tired of going around mountains. I want what God promised! I want to get involved with kingdom living in the here and now, not the hereafter. I desire to see some changes IN ME, in MY family, in MY church, in MY community." It is imperative we build up our Christian World Vision on the concept of God's Kingdom on earth. It is the centerpiece and primary focus of Biblical Christianity. What was the prayer Jesus taught His disciples to pray? I remind you again: *"Thy Kingdom come (where?) in earth as it is in heaven! (Matthew 6:10)*

Revelation 1:9-10, "I John, who also am your brother, and companion in tribulation, and in the kingdom and patience of Jesus Christ, was in the isle that is called Patmos, for the word of God, and for the testimony of Jesus Christ." Verse 10, "I was in the Spirit on the Lord's day, and heard behind me a great voice, as of a trumpet."

God has a plan that will work! That's good news. John declares in *Verse 9,* he was a companion in tribulation with us and stated that the Kingdom was present in his day, *"in the Kingdom and patience of Jesus Christ."* He states in *Verse 10,* he was in the Spirit and heard a GREAT VOICE (SHOUT) as of a TRUMPET. Is it possible to see the language of *I Thessalonians Chapter 4 Verses 16-17* in this last message to the church, which was not "go ye" but "repent." Repent means to change your mind. I declare to you that we will NOT see, understand, perceive or comprehend what John saw until we get where John was. And I'm not talking about the Isle of Patmos! Where was John? He was in the Spirit! Spiritual things are spiritually discerned (*I Corinthians 2:14*).

Jesus Came to Where John Was

Consider with me this train of reason and rationale. Futurists and rapturists tell us the first three chapters of *Revelation* deal with the church age, and in *Chapter 4, Verses 1 and 2* the "rapture" occurs for the church and is "CAUGHT AWAY" and not mentioned again. Let's read it right now. *Revelation 4:1-2, "After this I looked, and, behold, a door was opened in heaven: and the first voice which I heard was as it were of a trumpet talking* with me; which said, Come up hither, and I will show thee things which must be hereafter." Verse 2, "And immediately I was in the spirit: and, behold, a throne was set in heaven, and one sat on the throne." My friend, it doesn't say "caught away" but "come up." I submit for your consideration the language of I Thessalonians 4:16-17 bears a striking similarity to the language of the verses that you just read. Adding to this the words "first" and "voice" (SHOUT) as it were of a "TRUMPET" which said "come up here" (CAUGHT UP) do not signify the or a "rapture." Why do I say that? Because the verse in Chapter 1:10 has similar language (i.e. SHOUT, TRUMPET). We also would have to say the rapture occurred in Chapter 1 because John was in the Spirit. But where was John's body? On the earth, on an island. Even though John's body was on the Isle of Patmos, where was John's spirit? Caught up in the Holy Spirit's divine revealing. John never left the earth!! Jesus came to where John was. By His Spirit, God can come to where you are right now!

You see, John knew the flesh man, the human - Jesus. And he even saw the post-resurrected Christ. Ah, friend, John knew Him well. Wasn't he called the disciple whom Jesus loved? (John 13:23) But here on this island, in Patmos' inhospitable environment, John sees THE MIGHTY CHRIST he had never known before. He falls down before Him liken to a dead man (Verse 17). When we get a glimpse of the majestic many-membered Body of Christ radiating the effulgent GLORY of God, our response will be the same. Where did John the revelator see this glory? In heaven? No! This glory is to be revealed IN the EARTH, and it's not just "terra firma." You may ask, "What earth?" II Thessalonians 1:10-12 tells us that this pre-existent, ever-present, eternal glory is going to be exhibited (manifested). Do you have any inkling as to WHERE?!? this is going to happen? Read and get happy! Verse 10-12, "When he shall come to be glorified in his saints, and to be admired in all them that believe (because our testimony among you was believed) in that day." Verse 11, "Wherefore also we pray always for you, that our God would count you worthy of this calling, and fulfill all the good pleasure of his goodness, and the work of faith with power:" Verse 12, "That the name of our Lord Jesus Christ may be glorified in you, and ye in him, according to the grace of our God and the Lord Jesus Christ." When He (Jesus) shall come to be GLORIFIED IN HIS SAINTS" (in your earth), hold on a minute. Where is He going to be glorified? By the way, what are you made of? Dirt, dust. Genesis 2:7, "And the Lord God formed man of the dust of the ground." Let's start over with Verse 10-12. Read it slowly and prayerfully and then let the "eyes of our understanding be enlightened."

Are you aware that the word "glory" is mentioned 128 times in the New Testament? The Greek word is "doxa" which is the prefix in doxology. Ology, the suffix, means "the study of." I think we need to study a little bit more about this GLORY that John saw, and that Paul wrote about. Really, the "blessed hope" is NOT the unBiblical "rapture doctrine" that people so tenaciously hold on to, but rather *Colossians 1:27, "To whom God would make known what is THE RICHES OF THE GLORY OF THIS MYSTERY among the Gentiles, which is CHRIST IN YOU, THE HOPE OF GLORY."* (emphasis added).

Millions and millions of evangelical Christians are "paid up," "prayed up," and ready to "go up," but very few desire to fight the good fight of faith. You might say, "If I believe what you have written, it will cost me my reputation!" So what? It was spoken of Jesus *"he made Himself of no reputation." (Philippians 2:1)*

You might ask, "But I have so many friends that believe in the "rapture." How could so many people be wrong?" Sincerity has never been the litmus test for truth. Truth must at times stand alone, but we do have a Friend who sticks closer than a brother *(Proverbs 18:24)*. You are never alone, but you are still called to stand!

You may say, "Why, if I accept the position that you're setting forth, I'll lose my status as deacon, trustee or board member. I see truth in what you're sharing but I really do love my denomination. After all, our family has believed this particular rapture doctrine for years."

Do you know that the scripture deals with a scenario like this? It's the story of the man born blind whose parents loved the praises of men more than of God. And what's really hard to believe is, they were more afraid of losing their position in the synagogue than in standing up for their son who was blind from birth. Read *John 9:20-23, "His parents answered them and said, We know that this is our son, and that he was born blind:" Verse 21, "But by what means he now seeth, we know not; or who hath opened his eyes, we know not: he is of age; ask him: he shall speak for himself." Verse 22, "These words spake his parents, because they FEARED the Jews: for the Jews had agreed already, that if any man did confess that he was Christ, he should be put out of the synagogue." Verse 23, "Therefore said his parents, he is of age; ask him."*

The bottom line to this story is the tragic fact the religious leaders would have preferred to have the blind man continue in his blind condition than to see him healed. Even sadder still, so would his parents *(Verse 23)*, *"Therefore said his parents, he is of age; ask him."* If your heart and mind are being enlightened, then be prepared for the last 5 words of *Verse 34*,

"And they cast him out." But *Verse 35* tells us that Jesus waited until He heard that they cast him (the blind man) out. You see, Jesus goes looking and searching for the "outcasts." Isn't it ironic and incredulous, the blind man Jesus healed and could now see was cast out, disfellowshipped and ridiculed. Yet the Jewish leaders who said they could see, were really blind and sightless. They had cataracts on their hearts, despising the blind boy but loving their tradition. My, what darkness!

Please let me emphasize and accentuate the importance of seeing things with a spiritual mind. Without becoming pietistic, preposterous or puffed up, let us conclude this chapter with a list of prophets who told us how they received visions, prophecies and inspired utterances.

Numbers 24:2, "...and the Spirit of God came upon him..."
Judges 3:10, "And the Spirit of the Lord came upon him..."
Judges 6:34, "But the Spirit of the Lord came upon Gideon..."
(actually "clothed himself with" – Hebrew)
Judges 14:6, "And the Spirit of the Lord came mightily upon him..."
I Samuel 16:13, "...and the Spirit of the Lord came upon David."
II Chronicles 20:14, "...came the Spirit of the Lord in the midst of the congregation."
Isaiah 11:2, "...the Spirit of the lord shall rest upon Him..."
Isaiah 44:3, "...I will pour My Spirit upon Thy seed..."
Isaiah 61:1, "...the Spirit of the Lord is upon me..."
Ezekiel 3:12, "Then the Spirit lifted me up..."
Ezekiel 3:14, "So the Spirit lifted me up and took me away..."
Ezekiel 3:24, "Then the Spirit entered into me and set me upon my feet..."
Joel 2:28, "...I will pour out My Spirit upon all flesh..."
Zechariah 4:6, "...not by might, nor by power, but by my Spirit..."
Acts 2:4, "And they were all filled with the Holy Spirit..."
Acts 8:39, " the Spirit of the Lord caught away Philip"
Romans 15:19, "Through mighty signs and wonders, by the power of the Spirit of God..."
I Corinthians 14:2, "in the Spirit he speaketh mysteries"
Ephesians 5:18, "...be filled with the Spirit"
I Peter 1:22, "...obeying the truth through the Spirit"
Revelation 21:10, "...And He carried me away in the Spirit..."

Though the above scriptures are but a sampling of God's activity in the history of His people, I ask you, "Did these things really happen?" Are these promises still in force today? Has God abrogated His Word to be time specific for a former day only? I know Christianity is a thinking man's philosophy, but is it just cerebral? Can I emote? Can I really be CAUGHT UP in God's Spirit? Can I SHOUT? Did the walls of Jericho really, truly, come down when the people SHOUTED in 1413 B.C.?" Would your personality and austere reserve been embarrassed to join in the shouting when King David brought the Ark of the Covenant (God's Presence) back to the people of God? Or would you have despised David like Saul's daughter Michal when he danced before the Lord? The result of Michal's hypercritical attitude – barrenness the remainder of her life.

A critical, censorious attitude will shrivel and dry up the womb of praise, never to give birth, never to feel that kick of new life shut up in your belly that wants to come to full term. Didn't Jesus say in *John 7:37-39*, there was a river of life in your belly? In your innermost being? *"In the last dáy, that great day of the feast, Jesus stood and cried, saying, "If any man thirst, let him come unto me, and drink." Verse 38, "He that believeth on me, as the scripture hath said, out of his belly shall flow rivers of living water." Verse 39, "But this spake he of the Spirit, which they that believe on him should receive: for the Holy Ghost was not yet given; because that Jesus was not yet glorified."* Notice *Verse 39* tells us in unmistakable terms He was speaking of the Holy Spirit. Women who have given birth to children know that shortly after conception something different is going on inside them. Hormonal changes, chemical changes, emotional changes, dietary changes, food combinations that would never have been considered (pickles and ice cream, olives and peanut butter) are suddenly craved. As in the natural, so also in the spirit. When you get pregnant with truth, you crave a different diet. Your spirit and mind have been impregnated with the Word which is the incorruptible seed – *I Peter 1:23*. The Greek word for seed is spora, sperma. Amazing, isn't it?

A pregnant woman notices that regular clothes don't fit anymore. Have you ever said I can't fit into the sanctimonious suit of denominational dress? Why don't those clothes feel comfortable any longer? Answer: she's got new life in her, and after a while that new life will cause a certain illness called "morning sickness." I just can't eat religious rhetoric anymore. A pregnant woman becomes beautifully "awkward." She walks different. She's got a glow about her – a change of countenance. How else can we describe it? She's… she's… she's <u>expecting</u>!!! That's it! That's what we call it! Expecting!

I'm expecting also, and believing that the spirit of revelation and the knowledge of Christ will allow us to see that John the beloved experienced *I Thessalonians 4:16-17*. He was CAUGHT UP, heard the SHOUT and TRUMPET CALL to reveal to us more of Jesus and our Father's glorious purpose – His kingdom filling all the earth!

Chapter 14

King David – Caught Up In Majestic Praise

SHOUT, TRUMPET, CAUGHT UP in the Life of King David

What disappointment comes to a thirsty person when approaching a drinking fountain to see a sign attached to it "out of order." That which was originally designed and manufactured to dispense cold, refreshing water is of no use or value. It is out of order. It has all the looks of a working model, but something internal is non-functional. This is the great tragedy and pathos of man in this hour. Out of order! Have you become all that God destined you to become? Have you become conformed to God's Word? Are you yielding to the Holy Spirit? You were placed on the stage of life to be conformed to the image of Christ (*Romans 8:29*). Paul declares in *Galatians 1:15-16, "But when it pleased God who separated me...and called me by His grace" Verse 16, "To reveal His Son in me."* Think of it – to reveal His SON in ME! How absolutely glorious!

The intention of our Heavenly Father was <u>not</u> to reveal "the fallen Adam" but the "last Adam." Of course, we do bear the image of the earthy. The scripture in *I Corinthians 15:49* makes this abundantly clear. But it does not find its apex or zenith just in bearing the image of the earthy. Let's read *Verse 49, "And as we have borne the image of the earthy we <u>shall</u> also bear the image of the heavenly."* Can I only bear the image of the earthy on my terrestrial journey? Does the celestial encounter with the Eternal Covenant-keeping Mighty One of Israel give me the privilege of demonstrating the life of the

> **The Spirit of God urges you on to the deeper waters of truth.**

Father in the here and now? As children, surely we demonstrate the fallen Adam. We don't have to be taught to be selfish: it's inherent; it's natural. We want our own way. We want no accountability and no responsibility. Perhaps carnality reaches its full development when adolescence and teenage independence merge into the "know-it-all" phase of life, and this has nothing to do with chronological age. You could be 18 or 80.

As you aspire to the call of "sonship," the sophomoric attitudes of immaturity give way to the discipline of things dear to the heart of God. That which is dear to the heart of God is the issue that we must set forth in this hour. This is what King David felt as he returned the Presence of God to the people. In this chapter we shall attempt to return God's Presence to its rightful place.

97

Let me ask you a question. Was the ultimate intention of God in the life of David to kill the giant Goliath with a slingshot? Not really. It was part of his development but certainly not the high-water mark of his life's achievement. He was but a youth, a stripling, yet we thrill and with good cause, to admire reckless faith abandoned to the will of God. Can you feel the earth shudder and shake as the "stone of truth" hits Goliath in his carnal mind (right between his eyes) and his lifeless body staggers a few steps and crumbles to the ground? When did the Philistines know their champion was dead? As a matter of fact, when did the Israelites know Goliath was dead? Not when Goliath fell to the earth, but rather, *I Samuel 17:51* says, *"Therefore David ran and stood upon the Philistine and took his sword, and drew it out of its sheath and slew him, AND CUT OFF HIS HEAD* (emphasis added) *with it..."* We will know the enemy is dead when the "natural mind" can no longer operate.

It wasn't until David used the "sword" to cut off the "gigantic carnal mind" that the enemy no longer had power to control God's people and manipulate them through fear. Today the scenario is much the same. God's people are continually terrorized through the promotion of the monstrous antichrist giant in our day, as if that spirit is in control. One of the purposes of this writing is to take the stone of truth and by the Spirit's control, hurl it toward the head (carnal thinking) of antichrist dominant emphasis. Once the rejected stone (*Matthew 21:42*) hits its mark, the sword of the spirit (*Ephesians 6:17*) will eliminate the threats, taunts and thunder of a theology based on what the devil's doing. This day does not belong to Goliath, the Philistines, or the money merchants of Babylon, or even King Saul. This day belongs to Yahweh.

Isn't it amazing in this day: we trust our liberty to the lawyers, our health to the doctors, our money to the bankers, and our futures to a devil-dominated philosophy promoted by organized religion. Somehow, through applied progression we move beyond the reach of the shallow and superficial. The Spirit of God urges you on, and go to the deeper waters of truth.

Can you see that in the life of David? His rescuing the sheep from the lion and the bear were simply progressions of moving from faith to faith – strength to strength – glory to glory, to bring him face to face, not with Goliath, but face to face with God and His Kingdom? The real issue is God. He is the One David is to become acquainted with, because He is King and His Kingdom is what it's all about. Please don't let lions, bears or giants dominate our thinking, to get us off the central theme, which is God's Kingdom ruling and reigning supremely above and over all. This is the theme of the Bible.

In many of the previous chapters and Biblical accounts, we have found that where the words SHOUT, TRUMPET and CAUGHT UP are mentioned, there was battle and warfare. In this account in the life of King David, the same words are found but not in warfare, but rather "<u>WORSHIP</u>." That's why I questioned you earlier, to find out what the greatest accomplishments were in the life of David. Just look at his resume: Shepherd, warrior, psalmist, musician, poet, administrator, prophet, writer, worship leader and King to name a few. David had achieved it all, but I believe his crowning achievement was demonstrated when he restored the Presence of God to the people. Why do I say this? For the simple reason it was prophesied in the book of *Amos 9:11*. God was going to raise <u>up</u> in the *"last days"* the tabernacle of David, which was fallen down, and it was going to be built again. This text was quoted in the very first council within Jerusalem in *Acts 15:13-17, "And after they had held their peace, James answered, saying, Men and brethren, hearken unto me:" Verse 14, "Simeon hath declared how God at the first did visit the Gentiles, to take out of them a people for his name." Verse 15, "And to this agree the words of the prophets; as it is written." Verse 16, "After this I will return, and will build again the tabernacle of David, which is fallen down; and I will build again the ruins thereof, and I will set it up:" Verse 17, "That the residue of men might seek after the Lord, and all the Gentiles, upon whom my name is called, saith the Lord, who doeth all these things."*

Without going into a long detailed account by teaching on the subject of the *"tabernacle of David,"* let's just read the account as it is presented in *I Chronicles 15:1-3, 12-16, 25-29. Verse 1, "And David made him houses in the city of David, and prepared a place for the ark of God, and pitched for it a tent." Verse 2, "Then David said, None ought to carry the ark of God but the Levites: for them hath the Lord chosen to carry the ark of God, and to minister unto him forever." Verse 3, "And David gathered all Israel together to Jerusalem, to <u>BRING UP</u> the ark of the Lord unto his place, which he had prepared for it." Verse 12, "And said unto them, Ye are the chief of the fathers of the Levites: sanctify yourselves, both ye and your brethren, that ye may <u>BRING UP</u>* (emphasis added) *the ark of the Lord God of Israel unto the place that I have prepared for it." Verse 13, "For because ye did not at the first, the Lord our God made a breach upon us, for that we sought him not after the due order." Verse 14, "So the priests and the Levites sanctified themselves to BRING UP the ark of the Lord God of Israel." Verse 15, "And the children of the Levites bare the ark of God upon their shoulders with the staves thereon, as Moses commanded according to the word of the Lord." Verse 16, "And David spake to the chief of the Levites to appoint their brethren to be the singers with instruments of music, psalteries and harps and cymbals, sounding, by lifting* *up the voice of joy." Verse 25, "So David, and the elders of Israel, and the captains over thousands, went to <u>BRING UP</u> the ark of the covenant, of the Lord out of the house of Obed-edom with joy." Verse 26, "And it came to pass, when God helped the Levites that bare the ark of the covenant of the Lord, that they offered seven bullocks and seven rams." Verse 27, "And David was clothed with a robe of fine linen, and all the Levites that bare the ark, and the singers, and Chenaniah the master of the song with the singers: David also had upon him an ephod of linen." Verse 28, "Thus all Israel <u>BROUGHT UP</u> the ark of the covenant of the Lord with <u>SHOUTING</u>, and with sound of the cornet, and with <u>TRUMPETS</u>, and with cymbals, making a noise with psalteries and harps." Verse 29, "And it came to pass, as the ark of the covenant of the Lord came to the city of David, that Michal the daughter of Saul looking out at a window saw king David dancing and playing: and she despised him in her heart."* (emphasis added).

Do you see that these three significant words we have been emphasizing in *I Thessalonians 4:15, 17* are found here in a worship experience? Can you believe that a head of state, a dignified king would participate in such an undignified manner? Perhaps the Lord is telling us that we need to lose our dignity to gain our liberty. Where do you draw the line? Where are your limits when it comes to expressing worship? Could you do what David did? Shout? You answer, "I'm not sure." Playing the harp? That's not my gift! (*Verse 29*) Dancing? Who, me? You've got to be kidding.

David did all of these passionate things and did you know when he did them? Not when he was a youth, not a novice or beginner. At this occasion he was at the top of his career. After all, David was king; ruler over the realm. No one higher in the kingdom.

But I believe David was jealous. Jealous? Over what? Over the Levites. They composed the priesthood. They communed with God. They had the service of the sanctuary and that's what David wanted. Why, he even laid aside his kingly robe and crown and put on a linen ephod (*Verse 27*). That was the garment of the priest. Why, even in *Psalms 27:4*, David cries out *"<u>One thing</u> have I desired of the Lord that will I seek after that I may dwell in the house of the Lord all the days of my life, to behold the <u>beauty</u> of the Lord and to enquire in His temple."* He narrowed his life's pursuit to <u>one</u> thing. Can you? *Luke 10:42, "But ONE THING is needful: and Mary hath chosen that good part, which shall not be taken away from her."*

Are you aware that David was used to people bowing in his presence? He was accustomed to his subjects reverencing him with homage, honor and submission. Familiar to David were the blowing of <u>trumpets</u> announcing his arrival at significant events. <u>Shouts</u> of triumph and exultation from his constituents often sounded in his ears. People would rise up and stand on tiptoe to see the King and his royal entourage as he passed by.

Somehow most people today do not equate worship with dancing, leaping, trumpet blowing, or shouting, yet David laid aside his kingly embroidered garments, his jewel-studded crown and then danced in unbridled passion in celebration of the return of God's Presence to His people.

Isn't it criminal that we, God's people, can celebrate a sports event with applause and adulation but when it comes to the One who conquered death, hell and the grave we remain silent as a sphinx. What would happen if we would obey the admonition of the psalmist when he proposed in *Psalms 103:1, "Bless the Lord, Oh my soul, and ALL THAT IS WITHIN ME,* (emphasis added) *bless His holy Name."* Could you enter into that kind of worship? Could you rise above the criticism of those that would accuse you of emotionalism and fanaticism? David did!

What about *Psalms 132:9* which says, *"Let Thy priests be clothed with righteousness and let Thy saints SHOUT for joy?"* Somehow, the day came when David caught a glimpse of the grace of forgiveness and the desire of God to dwell in the heights of Zion. You see; Zion had been occupied by the Jebusites, the avowed enemies of God. Even though Israel had conquered the nations round about, the Jebusites had never been driven out of Zion, which was the highest part of Jerusalem. See *I Chronicles 11:4-9, "And David and all Israel went to Jerusalem, which is Jebus; where the Jebusites were, the inhabitants of the land."* Verse 5, *"And the inhabitants of Jebus said to David, Thou shalt not come hither. Nevertheless David took the castle of Zion, which is the city of David."* Verse 6, *"And David said, Whosoever smiteth the Jebusites first shall be chief and captain. So Joab the son of Zeruiah went first up, and was chief."* Verse 7, *"And David dwelt in the castle; therefore they called it the city of David."* Verse 8, *"And he built the city round about, even from Millo round about: and Joab repaired the rest of the city."* Verse 9, *"So David waxed greater and greater: for the Lord of hosts was with him."*

The great truth here is that where the highest realm of satanic activity dwelt, there the enemy is displaced through battle. And in that very spot where once the antagonists and bitter foes occupied and lodged, David through praise and worship pitched the Presence of God. Perhaps that's why in the New Testament Paul said, *"casting down imaginations and every high thing that exalts itself against the knowledge of God."* (*II Corinthians 10:5*).

The rendering of the Hebrew language is very graphic concerning this particular account in *II Samuel 6:14-15, "And David danced before the Lord WITH ALL HIS MIGHT* (emphasis added) *and David was girded with a linen ephod." Verse 15, "So David and all the house of Israel BROUGHT UP* (caught up) *the ark of the Lord with SHOUTING and with the sound of the TRUMPET."* (Notice the language of *I Thessalonians Chapter 4 Verse 16*.) This is the coming of the Lord to earth. David never left the earth. God came and dwelt with His people!

The statement, "with all his might," is rendered; David worshipped God in the undergarments of praise. You see David was really prophecying that God was going to uncover Himself with His bride, Israel, and be intimate in His love relationship with His national wife. After all, what did Michal, Saul's daughter accuse David of doing? She said he was lewd in his dancing for he danced so hard he uncovered himself. She accused him of being vile (*II Samuel 6:20*) and contemptible. What she failed to realize was that David was so CAUGHT UP in worship; prophetically he was birthing a new order of intimacy. David's tabernacle only had 3 sides to it. There was NO wall or veil. The people could see the Ark of the Covenant, which symbolized the very glory of God, the womb of worship. What a love story! Here God would dwell with his people and bring forth (beget, birth) sons of God. *John 1:14, "And the Word was made flesh and dwelt* (the Greek word for 'dwelt' is 'tabernacled') *among us, and we beheld His glory, the glory as of the only begotten of the Father, full of GRACE and TRUTH."* (emphasis added)

Jesus, thank you for pitching Your tent with the likes of us.

Chapter 15

Zechariah The Prophet – Caught Up In Prophecy

SHOUT, TRUMPET, CAUGHT UP
in the message of Zechariah the prophet

Zechariah was a prophet of restoration, revival and redemption. He, with prophetic vision, declared the betrayal of our Savior over 600 years before the occasion ever occurred and even told the amount – 30 pieces of silver (*Zechariah 11:12*).

Look at the list of other prophecies that this seer and sage revealed:

- His coming as the Prince of peace (*1:14-17*)

- The fullness of the Gentiles (*2:11*)

- The building of the temple of our God (*4:6-10, 6:12*)

- The priesthood of our Savior (*6:13*)

- Second coming of Jesus Christ (*8:2-3*)

- Messiah's reign (*8:4-8*)

- The restoration of the 12 tribes of Israel (*8:13, 9:1*)

- The Humanity of Christ (*9:9*)

- The Deity of our Lord (*10:4-6*)

- The restoration of the House of David (*13:1*)

- The Kingship of our Redeemer (*14:9*)

- The restoration of the Feast of Tabernacles (*14:16*)

These are just a few of the prophecies Zechariah deals with.

One of the significant truths to unfold about the prophecies of Zechariah is found in his name. His name means "God remembers." Our Heavenly Father doesn't have a case of amnesia, memory failure or forgetfulness. He has promised to restore and resurrect that which had fallen into ruin and obscurity. We have His Word to assure us these seemingly incredible impossibilities will certainly be forthcoming as we await patiently the promise. "He remembers."

Perhaps the most quoted passage of scripture from *Zechariah* is found in *Chapter 4:6*, "*...not by might, nor by power, but by my Spirit saith the Lord of hosts.*" When faced with a formidable foe or besieged by a belligerent antagonist, we rely on this promise and speak it audibly in faith. But are you aware of the question posed in the next verse? Read it aloud. *Verse 7, "Who art thou, Oh great mountain?* ("mountain" is symbolic for "kingdom") *Before Zerubbabel thou shalt become a plain: and He shall bring forth the headstone of it with SHOUTINGS, crying, Grace, grace unto it."*

Have you ever considered eliminating a mountainous problem by means of "SHOUT" therapy, especially when you're commanded to cry aloud, "Grace, grace" to it?"

The portion of *Zechariah* that deals with the words "SHOUT, TRUMPET, CAUGHT UP" is found in *Chapter 9. Verse 1, which* declares, *"all the tribes of Israel shall be toward the Lord."* I want to point out to you that the writer is not talking about the "Jews," but the whole house of Israel. (Go with me on a short scriptural journey.)

This was what Isaiah prophesied 200 years prior to Zechariah's statement in verse one. Read this prophecy from *Isaiah 49:5-7, "And now, saith the Lord that formed me from the womb to be his servant, to bring Jacob again to him, Though Israel be not gathered, yet shall I be glorious in the eyes of the Lord, and my God shall be my strength." Verse 6, "And he said, It is a light thing that thou shouldest be my servant to raise up the tribes of Jacob, and to restore the preserved of Israel: I will also give thee for a light to the Gentiles, that thou mayest be my salvation unto the end of the earth." Verse 7, "Thus saith the Lord, the Redeemer of Israel, and his Holy One, to him whom man despiseth, to him whom the nation abhorreth, to a servant of rulers, Kings shall see and arise, princes also shall worship, because of the Lord that is faithful, and the Holy One of Israel, and he shall choose thee."*

Can you believe that in *Verse 6* he states, *"It is a light thing to raise up the tribes of Jacob?"* Let me ask you further. In the New Testament, what was the Apostle Paul's defense before Agrippa? Was it not the same declaration of Isaiah and Zechariah? Read with me *Acts 26:6-7, "And now I stand and am judged for the hope of the promise made of God unto our fathers:" Verse 7, "Unto which promise our twelve tribes, instantly serving God day and night, hope to come. For which hope's sake, King Agrippa, I am accused of the Jews."* Paul said that the promise that was made to our fathers, was that Israel, the twelve tribes (not one tribe, the Jews or Judahites) but the twelve tribes, were instantly and earnestly serving God day and night. He then states at the end of *Verse 7* that the "Jews" are the ones accusing him.

These "Jews" were Babylonian Talmudic imposters (see *Revelation 2:9 and 3:9*). If they were part of Israel, then why would they be so upset at Paul? You see Paul was a "Jew" by religion but not by his tribe. What do I mean? Paul declares in *Philippians 3:5, "...of the stock of Israel, OF THE TRIBE OF BENJAMIN"* (emphasis added). Here he unequivocally states his tribal identity – a Benjamite! But he also states in that same verse that he was "a Pharisee." That answers the question about him being a "Jew." It was not his nationality but his "religion." And the religion of the Jews persecuted the Christians. They still do today! To verify this, look at *Galatians 1:13-14, "For ye have heard of my conversation in time past in the Jews' religion, how that beyond measure I persecuted the church of God, and wasted it:"* Verse 14, *"And profited in the Jews' religion above many my equals in mine own nation, being more exceedingly zealous of the traditions of my fathers."* Do you understand that Paul makes it abundantly clear in the first statement in *Verse 13* that it was the "Jewish religion" and his affiliation with it that made him a "Jew." There's a world of difference between a racial Judahite and a "religious Jew."

The reason I needed to make a differentiation between the two is simply this: part of the problem of the eschatology of futurism is that the "rapture" teaching is inextricably tied to the natural Jew in Palestine which has nothing to do with the true Israel of God! Let us proceed on and go to; SHOUT, TRUMPET and CAUGHT UP in the 9th *chapter* of *Zechariah*.

Separation at the Coming of the Lord

We are all desirous to know more about the coming of the Lord. Are you aware that one of the first priorities that occur at the setting up of the Kingdom will be the separation of the sheep (nations) and goats (nations)? *Matthew 25:31-34 states, "When the Son of man shall come in his glory, and all the holy angels with him, then shall he sit upon the throne of his glory:"* Verse 32, *"And before him shall be gathered all nations: and he shall separate them one from another, as a shepherd divideth his sheep from the goats:"* Verse 33, *"And he shall set the sheep on his right hand, but the goats on the left."* Verse 34, *"Then shall the King say unto them on his right hand, Come, ye blessed of my Father, inherit the kingdom prepared for you from the foundation of the world."*

> **Spiritual problems demand spiritual solutions.**

The goats are placed on the left hand and the sheep on the right. Notice what Jesus says, *"Come ye blessed of my Father inherit the Kingdom prepared for you from the foundation of the world."* So we learn that the following truths were established a long time ago. I share these scriptures for your consideration:

Read on...

- *Matthew 25:34... "Kingdom has been prepared from the foundation of the world... "*
- *Matthew 13:35... "secrets are being revealed that have been hidden from the foundation of the world... "*
- *Luke 11:50... "blood of the prophets was shed...from the foundation of the world... "*
- *Ephesians 1:3, 4... "we were chosen in Christ before the foundation of the world... "*
- *Hebrews 4:3... "works were finished from the foundation of the world... "*
- *Hebrews 9:26... "Jesus suffered from the foundation of the world... "*
- *I Peter 1:19,20... "the blood of Jesus was foreordained before the foundation of the world... "*
- *Revelation 13:8... "the Lamb was slain from the foundation of the world... "*
- *Revelation 17:8... "names were written in the Book of life from the foundation of the world... "*

I declare to you that the Kingdom of God is not an afterthought in the mind of God. He does not initiate plan "B" because plan "A" failed. Present day theology must depart from a fixation of antichrist-centeredness to Christ-centeredness – to Kingdom of God alignment within our hearts and minds. If our main focus is on anything other than Jesus and His ultimate intention, our theology will become weak. Why do you think we have such a weak and mild Christianity today? Perhaps we've been spending too much time trying to figure out what the enemy is doing instead of what our Heavenly Father has purposed.

A recent event proved this to be true. One of the men in our fellowship asked me to fill in for him at a noon luncheon at a local restaurant where after lunch a short devotional or Bible discussion was to ensue. To show you what I mean about us having a negative dominated viewpoint, I began the devotional with the scripture from *Matthew 24:37, "But as the days of Noah were, SO SHALL ALSO THE COMING OF THE SON OF MAN BE. "* (emphasis added). I then asked those gathered the question, "What was happening in Noah's day?" Let me ask you the same question. Before going on in this chapter, stop, hold your finger on this page, close the book and answer the question. What was happening in Noah's day? Please do this before reading on.

Well, was your answer much like theirs? One by one they responded, "violence filled the earth"; "they were eating and drinking"; "marrying and giving in marriage"; "the thoughts of men were only evil continually." Their replies were all negative and dissentient, which only proved my point. We have faulty theology because of flawed thinking. Have we ever asked our Heavenly Father, "Lord, what were you doing in Noah's day? God, were You doing <u>anything</u> in Noah's day?" Follow along with me in scripture and let's look at what God was doing!

Repeat with me the following: (I have included New Testament references for you to look up on your own). Remember this important fact, *"As it was in the days of Noah so shall it be at the coming of the Son of man."*

1. *Noah found grace in the eyes of the Lord (Genesis 6:8)*
   I find grace in the eyes of the Lord (Ephesians 2:8-9)
2. *Noah was a just man (Genesis 6:9)*
   I am a just man (Romans 5:1, 9)
3. *Noah walked with God (Genesis 6:9)*
   I walk with God (Colossians 1:10; I John 1:7)
4. *Noah was perfect in his generation (Genesis 6:9)*
   I am perfect in my generation (Matthew 5:48) (Say it by faith)
5. *Noah built an ark (Genesis 6:14)*
   I am building an ark (I Corinthians 3:9; Ephesians 2:21-22)
6. *Noah had household salvation (Genesis 6:18)*
   I have household salvation (Acts 11:14, 16:31)
7. *Noah released a dove (Genesis 8:8)*
   I release the Holy Spirit (the dove) *(Romans 5:5; John 14:26)*
8. *Noah built an altar (Genesis 8:20)*
   I am building an altar (Hebrews 13:10; Revelation 8:3-4)

Do you now see a greater and more powerful application of what God was doing in Noah's day? And also in ours? I suggest you repeat the above eight (8) statements of positive declaration until it gets from your brain to your bosom – from your head to your heart – from your thinking to your thanking.

I would at this point be candid and admit there was nothing wrong with the replies of the men at that noon luncheon, for the scripture does state exactly their quotes (*Matthew 24:38, "For as in the days that were before the flood they were eating and drinking, marrying and giving in marriage, until the day that Noah entered into the ark."*). We all know that it takes a storm to produce a beautiful rainbow. Therefore, through the negative behavior of an unbelieving world, let us positively proclaim the glorious message of the ultimate victory of our Savior and his glorious Kingdom. If in a world of darkness, you have a positive focus and as the scriptures say, *"an eye single to the glory of God,"* then remember this: *"a man with one eye is king in the land of the blind."*

Ramon Arias, a new acquaintance of mine, wrote me recently with a very cogent thought. He said, "We read in Genesis what was happening in Noah's days. We know that when Jesus prophesied the destruction of the temple, which took place in the year 70 A.D., He referred to the lifestyle and attitude of the people in Israel, at the coming of the Roman army, would be exactly as the ones in Noah's days."

He went on to say, "What God was doing in Noah's days was sanctioning the people who had corrupted themselves in a way that they left God no choice but to destroy them. So God was doing a two-fold action. First, He was removing the unjust from the world. Second, He was saving the just, Noah and his family, to continue with God's commission here on earth."

Sobering, isn't it?

As we proceed on in Zechariah, will you allow me to point out an important principle? And that is: there are some things you just cannot do. You cannot initiate salvation for we know that *"no man can come to the Father except the Spirit draw him."* Good works will not procure salvation for *"it's not of works lest any man should boast." (Ephesians 2:9)*. However, good works should follow salvation.

Things You Are Commanded To Do

The prophet Zechariah points out that there are some things you <u>CAN</u> do! In *Zechariah 2:7* he says, *"<u>DELIVER THYSELF</u> Oh Zion, that dwellest with the daughter of Babylon."* Do you understand that God is saying there is something that you have to do? Deliver yourself! In other words: "Get rid of Babylon's falsehoods; get rid of erroneous teachings; deliver yourself! There are some things that God says you must do!

As a matter of fact, what I am about to say is of great significance, not because I'm saying it but because it's historical importance is of your utmost consideration. Reflect with me on Peter's message on the day of Pentecost. It was the birthday of the church! God was initiating a new thing! 3,000 people were about to be born again! Jesus had promised Peter keys to the Kingdom *(Matthew 16:19)*. In *Acts, Chapter 2* the Holy Spirit was outpoured. From *Verse 14* through *Verse 40*, the scriptures contain the words that birthed the church. Peter was bringing to a conclusion this monumental message, and he ended it after the crowd was convicted in their hearts when they asked in *Verse 37 "Men and brethren what shall we do?" Verse 38, "Then Peter said unto them: Repent, and be baptized, every one of you in the Name of Jesus Christ for the remission of sins and ye shall receive the gift of the Holy Spirit." Verse 39, "For the promise is unto you, and to your children and to all that are afar off, even as many as the Lord, our God, shall call." Verse 40, "And with many other words did he testify and exhort saying, "<u>SAVE YOURSELVES</u>"* (emphasis added) *from this crooked generation."*

SAVE YOURSELVES – this was the first message that birthed the new creation. Peter concludes his message by saying; "SAVE YOURSELVES" from this crooked, convoluted and confused clergy! What else are we admonished to do?

- Consecrate yourselves – *Exodus 32:29*

- Sanctify yourselves – *Leviticus 11:44, 45*

- Separate yourselves – *Numbers 16:21*

- Present yourselves – *Deuteronomy 31:14*

- Set yourselves – *II Chronicles 20:17*

- Yield yourselves – *II Chronicles 30:8*

- Prepare yourselves – *II Chronicles 35:4*

- Examine yourselves – *II Corinthians 13:5*

- Comfort yourselves – *I Thessalonians 5:11*

- Submit yourselves – *James 4:7*

- Humble yourselves – *I Peter 5:6*

All of the above commands are placed in scripture for our growth, maturity and development. Spiritual problems demand spiritual solutions. There must be an answer to the divisiveness in the prophetic passages that we passionately defend. I'm not only searching the scriptures but admonishing you to do the same, and in concert with this, I am searching my heart. Why not take the popular position? I would prefer that, but that is not God's way.

Why Does God Make Me Uncomfortable?

Have you ever noticed when Adam partook of the tree of the knowledge of good and evil, that God <u>drove</u> him out of Eden? *Genesis 3:23-24, "Therefore the Lord God sent him forth from the garden of Eden, to till the ground from whence he was taken." Verse 24, "So he <u>drove out</u> the man;*

and he placed at the east of the garden of Eden cherubim, and a flaming sword which turned every way, to keep the way of the tree of life."

Adam didn't want to leave that pristine place. If you are holding onto traditions of men and fictitious premises and postulations, then be prepared to be shaken loose from the nest of comfort and complacency like the eaglets whose wise parents know when it's time for the young to try their wings and soar. The parents of that fledgling remove the down feathers that created a comfortable home for their young. Then with the pinions of its wings beating furiously, the mother makes it very uncomfortable for the young eagle to stay. Where once there was peace and solitude, now there is confusion and upheaval. What will God have to do to get you to fly? He will make things very uncomfortable for you. He will stir and drive you out of tradition.

The purposes and ways of God are past finding out. Can you see the mighty hand of God driving Jacob out from his family and familiar surroundings? He would never have had the dream of heaven's ladder extending from heaven to earth if he hadn't been driven by the mighty hand of God. With Almighty Yahweh above the ladder and Jacob with his head on a rock, our loving Father beckons his son to a new understanding of Come Up Higher! When Jacob awakened from his dream, his first statement was, "Surely God is in this place and I knew it not." (*Genesis 28:16*) Then Jacob did a very unusual thing. He took the stone he used for a <u>pillow</u> and set it up for a <u>pillar</u>. What happened next defies logic. Jacob poured oil on the top of it. As it was trickling down over the stone, Jacob uttered strange words. Was he aware of the prophecy that was coming out of his mouth that morning? Probably not. Nonetheless, out it came. He said, *"This is God's house...this is heaven's gate"* (paraphrase – *Genesis 28:17*). What? Jacob, are you saying that God's going to live in a stone Kingdom, a Kingdom people that have oil poured on them? Are you declaring that an anointed people are housing God's Presence? Jacob, are you aware you're laying a foundation stone for God to live in the earth?

Whether you knew what you did or not, Jacob, you did the right thing. You anointed the earth and said in effect, "God is going to live on the earth with us." Jacob, I'm so glad you prepared a foundation for us by pouring oil on that rock. If it were up to me, I would have tried to anoint that ladder to climb out of the earth realm, out of my difficulties, out of my problems; you know – escapism. But what God was saying was something like this: "Jacob, you anoint the earth and when you need me, there's a ladder extended from heaven to earth. I'll come down that ladder in the fullness of time (and He did – at Bethlehem!). In the meantime Jacob, what I'm looking for are a people that will anoint the earth. Jacob, if you will pour the oil on the earth, that ladder you saw in your dream will bridge heaven and earth. The angels that were ascending and descending will assist you in your earth experience to keep you wherever you go."

I ask you further, would Joseph have been willing to be sold as a slave into Egypt? God <u>drove</u> his brothers to betrayal not knowing that even in their wicked treachery they were providing for their own salvation. Somehow, what Jacob did as he poured oil on that stone years before, affected his young son Joseph. Joseph received an anointing to dream dreams like his father. And like his father, he too, would be driven out from his brothers. But also like his father, Joseph would anoint the earth. The fragrance of Joseph's life still blesses the earth. Let's turn our attention and focus to where Zechariah says God is moving – in the <u>earth</u>!

In *Zechariah 9:1-6,* Zechariah the prophet points out the coming of Christ and names nations and peoples who fight against the establishment of God's Kingdom on earth. In *Verse 1,* he identifies whom the covenant keeping people are (all the tribes of Israel) and declares their heart is going to be toward the Lord. He prophesies in *Verse 7* about a purging of speech and the infamy of lies will no longer be part of their vocabulary. Why don't we read *Verse 7, "And I will take away his blood out of his mouth and his abominations from between his teeth* (lies and untruths removed), *BUT HE THAT REMAINETH"* (emphasis added) (not raptured or taken away but REMAINETH) *"shall be for our God."* Do you see that it is essential for you to be "left behind" and "remain" to see the Kingdom?

No wonder *Verse 9* says, *"REJOICE GREATLY Oh daughter of Zion, SHOUT, Oh daughter of Jerusalem, behold Thy King COMETH UNTO THEE."* (emphasis added).

I know this verse deals with the first advent of our Lord but from *Verse 9* through the remainder of the book of *Zechariah,* the prophecies deal with the coming of the fullness of God's Kingdom. The first time our God came in the person of Jesus Christ, religious people were expecting and looking for a "physical kingdom" but our Savior and Redeemer brought them a spiritual one. In the second coming, religious people today expect and look for a "spiritual kingdom" but He's coming to receive a physical kingdom – right HERE on earth!

Verse 9 tells us to <u>SHOUT</u> – *"Rejoice greatly, Oh daughter of Zion"* (SHOUT).

Verse 11 identifies that the prisoners have been brought up (CAUGHT UP) out of the pit in which is no water. My own personal belief is that this identifies us as the children of Joseph. Look what is written of Joseph in

Genesis 37:23-24, "And it came to pass, when Joseph was come unto his brethren, that they stripped Joseph of his coat, his coat of many colors that was on him;" Verse 24, "And they took him, and cast him into a pit: and the pit was empty, there was <u>no water in it</u>."

Verse 12 encourages us to turn to the stronghold for we are prisoners of hope and that God is going to reward us "<u>double for our trouble</u>."

Verse 14 states the Lord Himself shall descend from heaven and BE SEEN over us... *"and the LORD GOD SHALL BLOW THE TRUMPET..."* (emphasis added)

The language of *I Thessalonians 4:16-17* is clearly shown in Zechariah's prophecies for those who have *"eyes to see and ears to hear."*

Chapter 16

Jeremiah Finally Rejoices – Babylon Falls

SHOUT, TRUMPET, CAUGHT UP in Jeremiah's Prophecies

The average modern day Bible believing church emphasizes two major messages: (1) die and go to be with Jesus; and (2) the doctrine of the rapture. No one in the real world wants to die. I heard of an older gentleman in a church service testifying that he was "homesick for heaven." The next day, after an examination by his doctor, he was notified that he had a terminal illness. All of a sudden, he wasn't as "homesick for heaven" as he thought he was. He paid the physician $15,000.00 for an operation so he wouldn't have to take the trip!

Jeremiah's message to the nation was about warning and judgment. No wonder he was termed "the weeping prophet." He propounded many unwelcomed truths about a coming captivity. His message was rebuffed and refused. He was imprisoned and fed the *"bread and water of affliction,"* but still his mission was pronounced in *Jeremiah 1:10*:

- to root out
- to pull down
- to destroy
- to throw down
- to plant
- to build

How would you like to have a ministry where two-thirds of it was negative in nature? Could it be that two-thirds of our belief system is faulty and needs to be destroyed and thrown down? This was the nature of Jeremiah's commission. No wonder the support and foundation of his calling is listed in the first chapter when Almighty God says in:

Verse 5, "I formed thee" and *"I knew thee"*
Verse 5, "I sanctified thee" and *"I ordained thee"*
Verse 7, "I shall send thee" and *"I command thee"*
Verse 8, "I am with thee to deliver thee"
Verse 9, "I have put my words in the mouth"
Verse 10, "I have this day set thee over the nations"
Verse 16, "I will utter my judgments"
Verse 18, "I have made thee this day a fortified city"
Verse 19, "I am with thee"

The Promise of a Fight

This kind of under girding and support will garrison your soul for the fight that God promises will come. You ask, "Does God promise a fight?" Listen as Jeremiah concludes the first chapter in *Verse 19, "And they shall fight against thee but they shall not prevail against thee; for I am with thee, saith the Lord, to deliver thee."* Although Jeremiah ministered to the house of Judah, they, by and large rejected his message. So he found he was received by a remnant. Has anything changed today? Are we to be discouraged because the majority of people fight against us? Not at all. Remember Jeremiah was promised a fight. I suppose one of the difficulties of ministry is that often it is not the enemies of God's people that oppose the work of the Kingdom but God's people themselves. Nonetheless, we must still declare the purposes of God.

> **The standard of success is not set by society but by God's Word.**

Jeremiah represented true leadership. The standard of success is not set by society but by God's Word. Real leaders are rare. They don't abuse power to satisfy egos. Godly leadership <u>always</u> tears down false images while displaying an example of right living. Because of a call to purity, true leadership destroys anything that would later tempt them from becoming all that they could become in God.

Jeremiah the prophet alerted the nation to the perils of the system of Babylon and told them they were going into captivity for 70 years and they would <u>not</u> escape or be "raptured out" of their difficulties or tribulations.

Jeremiah 25:8-11, "Therefore thus saith the Lord of hosts; Because ye have not heard my words," Verse 9, "Behold, I will send and take all the families of the north, saith the Lord, and Nebuchadnezzar the king of Babylon, my servant, and will bring them against the inhabitants thereof, and against all these nations round about, and will utterly destroy them, and make them an astonishment, and a hissing, and perpetual desolations." Verse 10, "Moreover I will take from them the voice of mirth, and the voice of gladness, the voice of the bridegroom, and the voice of the bride, the sound of the millstones, and the light of the candle." Verse 11 "And this whole land shall be a desolation, an astonishment; and these nations shall serve the king of Babylon seventy years."

The Bible warns us much about Babylon today as Jeremiah cautioned the nation of Judah in 650 B.C. You see; Babylon is a system of political, religious and economic parts, which in the New Testament is given the name, *"mystery Babylon." (Revelation 17:5).* This mysterious system has infiltrated and invaded every nation today even as it did the nation of Judah in Jeremiah's day.

Meeting Babylon – A "Head-On" Collision

My purpose is to appropriately warn you and also inform you that you are on a collision course with "mystery Babylon" and there is no avoiding or wishing it away. There is no rapture. Mystery Babylon wants control over your life, your family, your church and your nation. How do they implement their agenda? How do they impose their wicked rule? For us to comprehend their pernicious ways, let us look to a few salient verses in Jeremiah. The prophet declares a word against Babylon in *Chapter 50:1-2, "The word that the Lord spoke against Babylon and against the land of the Chaldeans by Jeremiah the prophet," Verse 2, "Declare among the nations and set up a standard, publish and conceal not; say Babylon is taken, Bel (or Baal) is confounded, Merodach is broken in pieces; her idols are confounded; her images are broken in pieces."*

First, the Lord speaks a word against Babylon. If God speaks a word against a nation, city or person, you can mark it down: that nation, city or person will NOT stand. The sure word of judgment will come to pass and it definitely won't be pretty.

As I have already mentioned, Babylon consists of primarily three parts: (1) political, (2) religious, and (3) economic. I shall address in brief form the religious aspect of "Mystery Babylon" and leave the political and economic aspects to be dealt with at a later time. There are no simple solutions to the problems we face. There's no magic wand to wave, no hocus-pocus, no quick fix. My desire in this writing is to turn human hearts one at a time and in the process, turn an escapist mentality that has been instrumental in neutralizing our churches and our culture. It can be done, but it will take patience and courage.

Who's to Blame? Religious Babylon

How did Jeremiah deal with the antagonists of his day? Where did he place blame? *Jeremiah 50:6* states, *"My people have been lost sheep, their __SHEPHERDS__* (emphasis added) *have caused them to go astray. They have turned them away on the mountains, they have gone from mountain to hill; they have forgotten their resting place."* Jeremiah declares that the blame lies with the clergy – the ministers – the preachers. This is part of religious Babylon.

Jesus addressed this exact same problem centuries later. When Jesus pronounced the seven woes, whom did he exonerate and reprove? Read

Matthew 23:13-36 and *Luke 11:46.* He singled out three groups of professionals: (1) the hypocritical clergy, (2) the scribes (writers and media persons), and (3) lawyers. These three groups contribute to the confusion we see today in religious Babylon.

Political Babylon

Jeremiah declares in *Jeremiah 50:17, "Israel is a scattered sheep, the lions have driven him away, first the KING* (emphasis added) *of Assyria hath devoured him and last this Nebuchadnezzar, KING* (emphasis added) *of Babylon, hath broken his bones."* This is political Babylon. The kings, the elite ruling class, the politicians all have devoured and swallowed up God's people. They have eaten their wealth through repressive taxation. Jeremiah had his "eastern establishment elite and military industrial complex" in his day too!

Economic Babylon

Jeremiah the prophet goes on to say in *51:7, "Babylon hath been a golden cup in the Lord's hand, that have made all the earth drunk; the nations have drunk of her wine; therefore, the nations are mad."* This is Babylon's economy – the golden cup filled with monetary success. *Chapter 51:13* goes on to state, *"O thou that dwellest upon many waters, abundant in TREASURES* (emphasis added) *thine end is come, and the measure of thy covetousness."* Financial Babylon is destined to fall as surely as the image that Daniel saw after it was hit by the stone of truth and was ground to powder (*Daniel 2:31-45*).

SHOUT, TRUMPET and CAUGHT UP in Jeremiah 51

In *Jeremiah 51:12-14* it says, *"SET UP the standard upon the walls of Babylon make the watch strong SET UP the watchmen* (come on, watchmen, get "caught up" in God's program), *prepare the ambushes; for the Lord hath both purposed and done that which He spoke against the inhabitants of Babylon." Verse 13, "Oh thou that dwellest upon many waters, abundant in treasures, thine end is come and the measure of thy covetousness." Verse 14, "The Lord of hosts hath sworn by Himself, saying, Surely I will fill thee with men as with caterpillars and they shall lift up a SHOUT against thee."* (emphasis added). (Here's that word, SHOUT!) Perhaps the shout of *I Thessalonians 4:16-17* won't only awake the dead, but also break down the walls of Babylon in the 21st century. In *Verse 12* God has purposes that His watchmen are "set up" (CAUGHT UP) and strong. They are prepared watchmen and *Verse 14* declares that they will lift up a SHOUT against Babylon.

116

Jeremiah 51:24-27 says, *"And I will render unto Babylon and to all the inhabitants of Chaldea all their evil that they have done in Zion in your sight, saith the Lord."* Verse 25, *"Behold, I am against thee, Oh thou destroying mountain, saith the Lord, that destroyest all the earth; and I will stretch out my hand upon thee, and roll thee down from the rocks and will make thee a burnt mountain."* Verse 26, *"And they shall not take of thee a stone for a corner, nor a stone for foundations, but thou shalt be desolate forever, saith the Lord."* Verse 27, *"Set up a standard in the land, blow the TRUMPET among the nations..."* The language of *I Thessalonians 4:16-17* is strikingly familiar to that in *Jeremiah 51*.

Babylon Has a Tummy Ache

Please notice that *Verse 34* shows that the Israel of God is no more seen because they have been devoured by the dragon - Babylon! *Verse 34, "Nebuchadnezzar the King of Babylon, hath devoured me, he hath crushed me, he hath made me an empty vessel, he hath swallowed me up like a monster, he hath filled his belly with my delicacies, he hath cast me out."*

What is Jeremiah prophecying? My, what powerful word imagery! He paints a word picture that describes death, burial, and resurrection. Why, it's the story of Jonah and the great fish that swallowed him up. Jonah was gone, finished, not to be seen, but wait, Jonah emerges as an obedient voice to declare the message of restoration. The whole capital city of Nineveh is spared and saved as a result of the mercy of God. Just as the great fish couldn't stomach the prophet Jonah, which represented truth, so also Babylon cannot hold in its belly God's people who have the truth of the resurrection. Read aloud *Jeremiah 51:44* and be blessed, *"And I will punish Bel* (Baal) *in Babylon and I will bring forth OUT OF HIS MOUTH* (emphasis added) *that which he hath swallowed up, and the nations shall not flow together anymore unto him: yea, the wall of Babylon shall fall."*

Babylon will no longer be able to hold on to that which it devoured; that which was swallowed up. The truth is going to be manifested and we will not be held hostage in the belly of the beast. Talk about tribulation! God's people have it backwards. We are the ones that give Babylon a bellyache! Babylon can't digest truth and the marvelous thought is, the enemies of the One who said "I am the way, THE TRUTH and the life," crucified and nailed TRUTH on an old rugged cross. TRUTH was taken down from the cross and entombed. Why, they even put the governmental seal of restriction on the tomb. Take a look and read what Pilate, the official voice of the most powerful earthly government, said to the chief priests and religious leaders who were afraid that TRUTH would be resurrected (*Mathew 27:65-66*). Pilate said unto them, *"Ye have a watch; go your way,*

117

make it as sure as ye can." Verse 66, "So they went, and made the sepulcher sure, <u>sealing</u> the stone and setting a watch."

I'm glad Pilate told them to make it *"as sure as ye can."* Why, they even set guards around it to make sure TRUTH would stay buried in the ground. However, TRUTH will prevail! It will come forth in resurrection power. Religious people can do their best to kill, destroy, stamp out, subvert and suppress TRUTH, but it will rise again. Why, that's its nature – not just to rise again, but with greater authority and power.

The Awesome Power of Truth

Didn't our Savior and Redeemer say in *John 12:24, "Verily, verily, I say unto you except a corn of wheat fall into the ground and die, it abideth alone, but if it die, it bringeth forth much fruit."*

Before Jesus died on the cross, the scriptures recorded that He raised people from the dead on at least three occasions: (1) Jairus' daughter, (2) the widow of Nain's son, and (3) Lazarus. Now, that is power! But the life that came after His death on the cross is <u>always</u> greater than the life that preceded His death. The next time He comes back, there will not just be three people raised from the death, but every person who has ever lived on planet earth. Now that is mega-power! That is resurrection power! That is the power of TRUTH!

Let us also die out to the opinions of men and the vanity of popular presumptions. "Heavenly Father, let TRUTH arise again in the hearts of your people. Resurrect then now, even though they are in Babylon's belly."

Dominus Vobiscum (The Lord be with you).

Chapter 17

Where Do We Go From Here?

The ultimate goal of this book is to establish in our hearts and minds God's righteous rule on this earth. Our Christian faith is extremely functional. We are not clinging to a hopeless gospel lifesaver to just keep afloat in a sea of conflicting opinions that breed despair. This is not a day for queasiness, double mindedness, or fence straddling. The only thing you get while straddling a fence is splinters. I hear people frequently say comments like, "I don't like controversy, I just want to stay in the middle of the road." Well, I've been down that road and the only things I see are yellow stripes and dead skunks.

> **Ask this to yourself. Does my viewpoint give the world hope?**

In this next to last chapter of this book, would you take a short trip with me? Come on, the car door is unlocked. Hop in and let's take a drive. As a matter of fact, here are the keys. Would you mind driving? There are four views I want you to consider as we travel the prophecy highway.

#1. The Spiritualist View

The first landscape I want you to look at on this drive is the Spiritualist view of prophecy. You see, as early as the days of St. Augustine of Hippo of the 4th century to our day today, some Bible students have proposed a theory that the book of Revelation was to show basic spiritual ideas and principles to be applied inwardly and introspectively. Basically, that's it.

The proponents of this view do not see a forecast of future events but simply the ultimate triumph over evil. May I submit to you that if you only look within, you'll be missing the scenery and grandeur of God's majestic purposes and worse yet, you will not have your eyes on the road and unfortunately, you could wreck my car. Could you pull over to the side of the road to let all those "futurists" get by. They sure are in a hurry to get to the "land of tomorrow." For the futurist, the answers to prophecy are always around the next bend in the road. They are notorious for setting dates for prophetic fulfillment of future events and when they don't come to pass, they even extend the day by months or years so they can market and sell their next book. For the most part concerning purchasing a book on futuristic prophecy, I have some advice. Keep your money in your pocket, wait 6 months and there will be another prophecy expert setting yet another date still off in the future.

#2. The Futurist View

Earlier in this book, I gave a thumbnail sketch and brief history of some of the proponents of this view. This interpretation declares that the first three chapters of *Revelation* were completely fulfilled during the time in which the seven churches in Asia Minor existed. Although the messages to the churches are to be applied spiritually, they also conclude that the treatises are to be looked at with an understanding of what was spoken to the seven church ages.

Pastor and teacher Charles Jennings, author of "The Book of Revelation" (from an Israelite and Historicist Interpretation) states concerning the futurist view, and I quote, "The pre-tribulationists which hold strongly to this view based their interpretation in regard to the fulfillment on the "Gap Theory" (Gentile Church age) regarding the 70th week of Daniel as found in *Daniel 9:25-27*. Two major beliefs of the pre-tribulation futurists are: (1) that the seven churches represent seven church ages dating from the first century until now with each respective church age fulfilling the description of the characteristics which Christ gave to each church; and (2) that the door which was open in heaven, seen by the Apostle John in *Revelation 4:1*, refers specifically to a pre-tribulation secret rapture of the church." (end quote).

O.K, I think we're ready to resume our journey down the prophecy highway. But before you pull out into traffic, do you mind checking the rear view mirror to see that we don't get run over by those frenzied, fast-paced futurists?

#3. The Preterist View

This position prophetically is what I term the rear view mirror theory or hypothesis. The word "preterist" basically means "past," so this viewpoint tries to prove that the Book of Revelation referred to contemporary events that culminated with the destruction of the Temple in Jerusalem and subsequent events that took place within the first century Roman Empire. Adherents to this view believe that the Book of Revelation has come to a state of fulfillment in past history and most proponents do not permit further consummation of a "progressive historical" view. May I remind you that this is a very brief encapsulation of these views, for there are "partial" preterists and "full" preterists with every hue and color in between. The one significant point I do wish to make is that they look back (rear-view mirror) to 70 A.D. as to the coming of the Lord.

Now, it is good to know that we do have a rear-view mirror to show God's faithfulness with significant monuments to fulfilled prophetic passages.

However, you really should be alert to what's around you and what's ahead to determine where you're going. It's wonderful to look back but while driving my car, don't look back all the time or we're going to have a wreck. Let's go. Accelerate!

#4. The Historicist or Historical View

This view postulates that the Book of Revelation predicts events occurring from the 1st century up to our present day. This view, according to many theologians and reformers of the past, offers a freedom in the interpretation of the text in applying the prophecies to actual historical events that have taken place from the 1st century. The historical position looks at Church history from the time of John the revelator to the culmination of all prophetic events, some even yet future.

It is very important to note that many reformers, men of God, teachers and Bible translators and scholars taught this position concerning Bible prophecy. Many of the men on the following list did not agree on certain doctrinal beliefs, but they were all in general agreement concerning the interpretation of Daniel's seventy weeks identifying the beast system as religious papal Rome and the "man of sin" being none other than the Roman popes who had taken the name Vicar of Christ.

Here's a partial list of those who subscribed to the "historicist view" of prophecy:

John Wycliffe, 1329-1383 – English "Morningstar of the Reformation"

John Knox, 1514-1572 – Scottish Presbyterian reformer

William Tyndale, 1494-1536 – English reformer, translator, martyr

John Calvin, 1509-1564 – French reformer and theologian

Martin Luther, 1483-1546 – German theologian and reformer

Ulrich Zwingli, 1484-1531 – Swiss reformer

Philip Melanchthon, 1497-1560 – Composed the Augustine confession

Sir Isaac Newton, 1642-1727 – English scientist and Bible scholar

John Huss, 1373-1415 – Bohemian reformer

John Foxe, 1516-1587 – English author of Foxe's Book of Martyrs

Charles Wesley, 1708-1788 – English hymn writer

John Wesley, 1703-1791 – Founder of Methodism

Jonathan Edwards, 1703-1758 – American theologian

George Whitfield, 1714-1770 – English evangelist

Charles Finney, 1792-1875 – American evangelist

Charles H. Spurgeon, 1834-1892 – English Baptist pastor

Adam Clarke, 1762-1832 – Methodist theologian

Matthew Henry, 1662-1714 – Welch Bible scholar

John Bunyan, 1628-1688 – Puritan author of Pilgrim's Progress

Hudson Taylor, 1832-1905 – English founder of China Inland Mission

F. B. Meyer, 1847-1929 – English Baptist preacher

Reading the names of these notable God-fearing men should cause us to search out why they believed this prophetic viewpoint. We cannot casually dismiss their approach to prophecy while embracing the position of Reformed theology that they propounded, which has stood the test of time.

An evangelist and teacher that preached a reformed theology and a gospel message 60-70 years ago in North Carolina was named Mordecai Ham. He subscribed to the historicist view of prophecy. His name doesn't ring a bell with most folks today, but one of his converts has name recognition all over the world. Yes, Billy Graham came forward to pray the sinner's prayer in Dr. Ham's meeting.

Say, thanks for the brief ride we took on the prophecy highway. Now let me tell you what I believe. You ask, "Do you subscribe to the "Spiritual" view of prophecy?" I would have to say, "Yes, about 10% of my viewpoint would include the valid interpretation of the introspection and looking within."

"Well," you ask, "what about "Preterism?" Do I believe that prophecy was fulfilled in 70 A.D. with the destruction of the temple in Jerusalem by the Roman general Titus? Why, of course I do! And this view of prophecy also has validity. So here are another 10-15% of my convictions concerning prophecy. But I do not want to spend all my time looking back to the 1st century of Christianity.

"O.K., let's see if there is anything about futurism that you can agree or accede validity to," you may ask. Why sure, I believe that history is an unfolding of God's great majestic plan. I believe that the best is yet to be. I believe there is no Kingdom without the King. Are there events and prophecies yet to be fulfilled? Why, sure! But it's not relegated to just a seven-year time frame. This futurist view incorporates about another 10% of my theological position.

About 70% of my belief system of prophecy is tied to a climactic, historical sovereignty of God position.

I think it's important to ask yourself some questions:

- Does my viewpoint give the world hope?

- Is my position utter destructionist?

- Does my view harmonize with the covenants?

- How do I deal with the Zionist state of Israel?

- Does my position abdicate my responsibility to change our culture?

These questions and many others must be answered for our generation.

Our great covenant keeping Yahweh promised to bless all the families of the earth by using one man and his family – Abraham and his seed (*Genesis 12:1-3; Genesis 13:15; Genesis 15:4-6; Genesis 17:4-8, 19; Genesis 22:17-18; Genesis 24:60; Genesis 26:24; Genesis 27:28-29; and Genesis 28:10-15*).

This isn't just the spiritual seed of Christ (*Galatians 3:16-19*) but Abraham had a natural and national seed with lands to inherit (*Romans 4:13*). His offspring became many nations and kings, although the theological world would have us believe that God just discarded and threw away His promises to the whole House of Israel. It seems so many people believe that every natural promise, every physical blessing is given to a racial group that call themselves Jews.

I can assure you that the scattered tribes of Israel were not so insignificant that God would just eliminate them from His covenant promises and purposes (*Jeremiah 31:31; Hebrews 8:8-9*). The fact that the sun came up this morning assures me that the promises and prophecies made to Abraham are being fulfilled and even now present in the earth, though we may be blind to this truth. Let me leave you with a question to ponder…where were your ancestors and what was their language and culture about the time of Christ, when Jesus walked the earth? You may not have any way of knowing for sure, but God Almighty was working through history to bring you to the Kingdom for such a time as this.

Our wise and living Father, in drawing up His Plan
To initiate His purpose, to enfold it within man,
Brought His Glory from the heavens where joys celestial flow,
Established beauty in a garden where this glory now can grow.
In scintillating brilliance, in majesty divine,
Adam was created in the fullness of God's time.
Our Father longs for fellowship, and love responding still;
He doesn't want just servitude, worship flows from man's free will.
This family life was shattered and was broken by man's sin;
Adam's life a failure and most think God can't win.
But His purposes move onward, He's not dismissed His Plan;
His glory's yet to be revealed though thwarted by this man!
All heaven bowed in silence and not a sound was heard,
Wisdom called to mercy and God brought forth this word:

"I'll have sons and daughters too, for that is My desire,
not bond but free, not serfs or slaves, nor those put out for hire.
First Adam's sin and brokenness, now God's second phase begun;
He took His finest glory and poured it in His Son.
This time I'll take My glory, I'll wrap it up in shame.
This Son will manifest My grace, He'll heal the sick and lame;
And on a cruel rugged cross He'll give His life for man,
Adam's race once fallen, restored to Me again."

Some say this plan's not working, they focus on what's heard;
What's seen is what's important, losing sight of God's own Word.
But He'll take your shame, your broken life, misunderstanding too,
Things so grotesque, things you despise, He'll make your life brand new!
Our God is filled with wisdom, O praise His precious Name!
For glory opened wide its mouth and swallowed all our shame!

Chapter 18

Concluding Remarks

For those of you that enjoy an in-depth study of the Word of God and not just a casual glance, I have provided two charts on the next pages for your continued examination. I would point out the first chart validates those who believe in the baptism of the Holy Spirit with the manifestation of glossalalia, better known as "speaking in unknown tongues." As you know, the scriptures declare that we need two or three witnesses to establish a biblical matter (*Numbers 35:30, Deuteronomy 17:6, Matthew 18:16, II Corinthians 13:1*). The same is true for doctrinal truths and Biblical experiences.

If you believe in a "Pentecostal experience" you have adequate Biblical support for your position according to God's Word. The heading of the first chart is "The Infilling of the Holy Spirit." The scriptural references are listed on the left-hand column of the page so they will be easy for you to find in your Bible. The chart is self-explanatory.

There are only three (3). I repeat, only three times in scripture that "tongues" are a sign, evidence or proof of the infilling of the Holy Spirit. Yet I believe that this gift is a viable, reasonable, rational, legitimate Biblical experience. Why? Because we have the required three witnesses of scripture. Those of you that are "Pentecostal" can search all you want but you base your experience on those three specific texts that mention tongues as a sign.

With that thought in mind, let me assert that on the second chart I have listed twelve (12) examples where the words "SHOUT, TRUMPET and CAUGHT UP" are found in your Bible. Don't you think that it would be in your best interests to search the scriptures to verify and validate these (12) examples in the light of the religious world's pre-occupation with the "rapture" teaching? I pray that the Holy Spirit, which was given to lead and guide you into all truth (*John 14:26*) will bless you abundantly in your search of unfolding insight in God's Word. May you also say when finished with your quest for truth, "I WANT to be Left Behind" to inherit the Kingdom prepared for me from the foundation of the world."

*May God's love, grace and mercy sustain us
through the power of His precious blood.*

"te Diem laudamus" (We praise Thee, O God)

Appendix A

The Infilling Of The Holy Spirit

Chart #1

Text	Relationship Word(s)	Observable Phenomenon	Effects of Being Filled (What Happened)
John 20:22	"receive ye"	Jesus breathed on them	None recorded
Acts 1:8	"come upon"	Nothing mentioned	Ye shall receive power
Acts 2:2-4	"all filled"	Heard rushing wind; saw tongues of fire	Spoke with other tongues
Acts 8:14-18	"they received"	Verse 18: Simon saw something he wanted to buy	None recorded
Acts 9:17	"be filled"	Healing; sight restored	Verse 20: Boldness to preach
Acts 10:44-47	"fell on"	Spoke in tongues	Magnified God
Acts 11:15-17	"fell on"	None recorded	None recorded
Acts 19:1-6	"came on"	Tongues and prophecy	None recorded

Appendix B

Scripture References for
"SHOUT." "TRUMPET," "CAUGHT UP"

Chart #2

Reference	"SHOUT"	"TRUMPET"	"CAUGHT UP"
I Thessalonians 4:16-17	Verse 16	Verse 16	Verse 17
Exodus 19:11, 16-20	Verse 16	Verse 19	Verses 17, 20
Joshua 6:2-5, 20	Verses 5, 16, 20	Verses 4, 5, 20	Verses 5, 20
I Chronicles 15:3-29	Verse 28	Verse 28	Verses 3, 7
II Chronicles 20:1-29	Verse 19	Verse 28	Verse 16
Psalms 47:1-9	Verses 1, 5	Verse 5	Verses 3, 8
Jeremiah 51:1-44	Verse 14	Verse 27	Verses 1, 44
Joel 2:1, 11; 3:7, 9	Chapter 2:11 Chapter 3:16	Chapter 2:1	Chapter 3:7, 9
Amos 1:2; 3:6; 9:11	Chapter 1:2	Chapter 3:6	Chapter 9:11
Zechariah 9:1-17	Verse 9	Verse 14	Verse 16
II Corinthians 12:1-4			Verse 4
Revelation 1:9-10 Revelation 4:1-2; 5:2	Chapter 4:1 Chapter 5:2	Chapter 1:10 Chapter 4:1	Chapter 4:1